Earth and Beyond in Tumultuous Times

Future Ecologies Series

Edited by Petra Löffler, Claudia Mareis and Florian Sprenger

Earth and Beyond in Tumultuous Times: A Critical Atlas of the Anthropocene

edited by

Réka Patrícia Gál and Petra Löffler

µ meson press

Bibliographical Information of the German National Library
The German National Library lists this publication in the Deutsche Nationalbibliografie (German National Bibliography); detailed bibliographic information is available online at http://dnb.d-nb.de.

Published in 2021 by meson press, Lüneburg, Germany
www.meson.press

Design concept: Torsten Köchlin, Silke Krieg
Cover image: Mashup of photos by Edgar Chaparro on Unsplash and johndal on Flickr
Copy editing: Selena Class

The print edition of this book is printed by Lightning Source, Milton Keynes, United Kingdom.

ISBN (Print): 978-3-95796-189-1
ISBN (PDF): 978-3-95796-190-7
ISBN (EPUB): 978-3-95796-191-4
DOI: 10.14619/1891

The digital editions of this publication can be downloaded freely at: www.meson.press.

Contents

Series Foreword: Future Ecologies

Edited by Petra Löffler, Claudia Mareis, and Florian Sprenger

The future of life on Earth has generated ongoing debates in academia, through which the concept of ecology has gained status by being able to connect disciplines across the natural sciences, humanities, arts, design and architecture. Criticism of the effects of climate change, which exacerbate existing inequalities in our global population, has spread from academia to the political and public spheres. At a time when the future of life on this planet is more uncertain than ever, the urgency of exploring other ways of thinking, acting and dwelling together is evident. This book series investigates emerging ecologies in uncertain worlds—ecologies that are open to the interests of other-than-humans and that care for plural modes of existence. By providing a platform for these topics and debates, we hope to contribute to a nature contract with the Earth as the shared common ground of water and minerals, air and birds, earth and woods, living and non-living, active and passive matter.

Future Ecologies is about a "time-space-mattering" that calls into question common knowledges about the relationship between space, place, territory, and the linearity of time in light of the circulation of matter, energies, and affect. It also questions the meaning of past ecologies and unsustainable futures for emergent ecologies, while problematizing the ambivalent histories of environmental knowledge, especially in the interplay of modernity and coloniality. Reading research in the *Future Ecologies* series allows you to take the many facets of past ecological thinking into account, to reveal its differentiated and often contradictory political implications and effects—and to criticize its, sometimes, naïve promises. Studying *Future Ecologies* means not taking for granted what ecology means.

The series promotes a relational thinking that is aware of the environmental, economic, social, and individual complexities of such a pluriverse driven by equally complex technologies and infrastructures. As Donna J. Haraway said, in a shared world "nothing is connected to everything, but everything is connected to something". This connection generates and discloses different scales of responsibility. We dedicate this book series to all earthly critters who want to invent and try out new forms of life and styles of cohabitation, who ask which risks we want to and are able to take, and which futures we dream of. We invite contributions that address the geopolitical inequalities of climate change and capitalist extractivism, that deal with politics of (un)sustainability and (de)futuring, technologies of recycling and environing, non-anthropocentric epistemologies and practices of world-making.

The *Future Ecologies* series advocates for interdisciplinary approaches towards the numerous aspects of ecology. We invite junior and senior scholars from various disciplines in media, cultural and literary studies, anthropology, design, architecture, and the arts to build collaborations between different voices, practices and knowledges—that is: heterogeneous communities of practice. By endorsing open access publishing, the series also aims to partake in the current transformation of the ecologies and economies of knowledge production.

Caucho

Mátyás Sirokai

Those who work with metal resemble metal. Metals hold the power over bodies. Those who work with stone resemble stone. Stones hold things of the past. Yet if you want not power but momentum, you desire not what's been but what's to come, then work with flexible materials, as these are embodiments not of mineral, but organic strength.

Those who take the caucho path then,
do it for the pleasure of flexibility, for the bounce and for the storage of energy, for the momentum not wasted. For the hands which clapped on the caucho for the first time.
For the hands which come to resemble the caucho. For the hands which first began to play with it. For the tree which can't. And for the grievers comforted by the game.

Translated by Owen Good

[1]

Introduction

Réka Patrícia Gál and Petra Löffler

Siting and Citing

There is more than one "Anthropocene." The concept was popularized at the start of the millennium by atmospheric chemist Paul Crutzen and biologist Eugene Stoermer (2000) to denote a new geological epoch characterized by unprecedented human influence over "nature," but the varying terminology that has been used to refer to it has become subject to intense debate across the board in the sciences, humanities, and arts. The word has generated numerous corresponding and opposing neologisms—Capitalocene (Moore 2015), Chthulucene (Haraway 2016), Plantationocene (Haraway 2015), and Thanatocene (Bonneuil and Fressoz 2016) among others—which focus on the importance of capitalist-colonial extractivism and racist knowledge, as well as material, production in the emergence of this proposed new geological epoch. In consequent debates, the assumption of a universal *anthropos* (Pálsson et al. 2013) has been criticized because of its inherent privileging of the Western subject.

As these debates demonstrated, confronting the Anthropocene requires a radical onto-epistemological shift that removes the Western subject (Hall and Gieben [1992] 2011) from its previously established position of standing separate from, and above, nature. The concept demands that we revise the long-established divides between humans and nature, global and local, living and inert, and that we develop new relationships with the spaces in which we live and of which we dream, from the manifold landscapes of the Earth's surface all the way to outer space. Breaking away from these axiomatic divides necessitates the acceptance of values and interests of diversified non-humans, as well as the rejection of traditional notions of technological progress, hierarchized knowledge systems, modes of individualization, and assumptions about human superiority. It requires that we actively work against Western anthropocentrism and the over-representation of capitalist economies and colonial knowledge production in politics as well as in science and art, while foregrounding multispecies and dynamic material entanglements in academic debates and beyond.

The aim of *Earth and Beyond in Tumultuous Times* is to contribute to the important work being done in this field that decenters and overcomes privileged perspectives on the planetary environment and its relations with outer space. This work takes place in and responds to a time of massive ecological crisis—that is, of climate change, mass extinction, environmental degradation, and their cumulative, far-reaching causes and effects on the social, political, and economic spheres. In order to do this, our volume approaches the Anthropocene as a boundary object, the investigation of which inherently necessitates an interdisciplinary approach and sharing of knowledge. Boundary objects are used in different communities of practice simultaneously to produce a shareable understanding; they are plastic and robust at the same time, able to "adapt to local needs ... yet ... maintain a common identity" across their various sites (Star and Griesemer 1989, 393).

This introductory chapter situates the timing and placing of the Anthropocene in various scholarly traditions and trajectories. In tracing the influence of the concept on the fields of environmental history, critical geography, media geology and ecology, as well as science and technology studies, we are committed to a *thinking with care*, "a distinctive style of connected thinking and writing that troubles the predictable academic isolation of consecrated authors by the way it gathers and explicitly honors the collective webs one thinks with rather than using others' thinking as a 'background' against which to foreground one's own" (Puig de la Bellacasa 2017, 76–77). Doing so allows the contributors not only to think with other scholars from different disciplines and academic backgrounds, but also to honor non-human agents such as rivers, corals, and ants, while admitting that knowledge production is always partial and situated in place and time as well as being affected by different interests and constraints (Haraway 1988; Stengers 2010).

The project of this volume, as it has grown out of the intellectual, artistic, and ethical commitments of the "Atlas of the Anthropocene" symposium, held in June 2018 at the Humboldt University of Berlin, is founded upon the very idea of such entangled thinking and is committed to interdisciplinary inquiry and the promotion of young researchers in order to foster transversal collectives of knowledge makers. Supporting emerging researchers and bringing them into conversation with established scholars provides space for knowledge production to be cultivated through connection and engagement. In this introduction, we hope to help situate readers spatially and temporally in the shifting grounds of our interconnected and interdependent existences to clarify where we are standing and who we are thinking with. We argue that centering how the scholarly understandings of space, territory, habitat, milieu, and the place of humans and non-humans within these evolved is in fact foundational to interpreting the scientific discourses of dwelling on Earth and beyond. In so doing, we focus especially on attempts to unsettle privileged perspectives and decolonize epistemologies of the Anthropocene (Mignolo 2011).

Appropriating space, claiming a place, and mapping a territory are colonial practices within different scales and time frames (Said 1993). The scaling of space and time produces power relations and knowledge formations and is thus always political. We intend to think with decolonizing knowledge practices in order to investigate both practical and theoretical landscapes and depths from plural and non-totalizing perspectives. We agree with historian José Rabasa that "the totality of the world can never be apprehended as such in a cartographical objectification, maps have significance only within a subjective reconstitution of the fragments" (1995, 360). Our volume therefore aims to incorporate plasticity into its structure and use it to our advantage.

Atlases and maps have historically served a violent homogenizing function. Subverting their dominant characteristics can be a powerful tool to visualize alternative ways of world-dwelling. Simryn Gill's unimposing sculpture entitled "Four Atlases of the World and one of Stars" (2009, paper, glue) is a good example in this respect. The artist arranged five small paper balls made of torn up and reassembled pages from atlases on a platform. These atlases are no longer flat scientific representations of a territory—instead they are more or less regular spheres in close spatial relation to each other resembling a volatile and random assemblage of balls in a children's game. Shaped as spheres, the atlases are not important instruments of geopower; rather they are light bodies that matter because of the relations between them. Gill's paper balls create a constellation, or better a "chaosmos" of possible worlds, to adopt a term by Félix Guattari (1992), seemingly fulfilling art historian Georges Didi-Huberman's description of the atlas as "a tool, not the logical exhaustion of possibilities given, but the inexhaustible opening to possibilities that are not yet given" (2018, 5).[1]

[Fig. 1] Simryn Gill: Four Atlases of the World and one of Stars (Source: Detail of an installation shot by Eike Walkenhorst from the exhibition *Down to Earth: Klima – Kunst – Diskurs unplugged*, Berlin 2020)

Our volume is dedicated to such a making-possible of worlds that are not yet given or are not honored, but that are necessary for imagining and fighting for both on Earth and beyond—worlds as small and inert as paper balls, or as big and vivid as deep-sea habitats. Towards this goal, each article in our volume provides analyses of a fragment of our geographical, stratigraphical, and theoretical landscapes and sheds light on often-ignored viewpoints, which, when read together, should provide a non-totalizing, imperfect, yet critical, "atlas" of the Anthropocene.

1 Stefanie Hessler (2020, 95) refers to Didi-Huberman's poetic description in her contribution to the booklet of the exhibition "Down to Earth: Klima – Kunst – Diskurs unplugged" that took place at Martin Gropius Bau in Berlin (August 13 to September 13, 2020).

The epistemological restrictions of maps and atlases become apparent when Indigenous technologies of wayfinding, such as stick charts from the Pacific, come into view. Narrations too, can be powerful counterparts to Western cartography. They are also crucial for a critical understanding of the Anthropocene's suggested time frame. This is why we start our volume with two contributions that question the hegemonial narrative of the Anthropocene from the perspective of the colonized "Global South." Tomás Usón's article discusses how the differing memory practices and knowledge regimes of Western sciences and Peruvian locals of the Ancash region ultimately lead to divergent interpretations of climatic catastrophes and, therefore, of the allocation of responsibilities and resolutions. Usón uses the concept of "boundary objects" (Star and Griesemer 1989) to reflect on human actors with diverse ontological backgrounds and world arrangements; he introduces the idea of ontological disputes in order to connect different memory regimes and legal systems. In the same vein, Jörg Dünne sheds light on the shifting treatment of geologic time in Argentinian fiction, from the usage of geological time as foundational to nationalism to its deployment as emblematic of environmental-political violence. In particular, he regards the fluvial environment of riverscapes as thresholds where different time scales collide and new communities of experience emerge.

Jakob Claus' contribution contrasts the cybernetic perspective on a technologically manageable and programmable Earth prominently privileged in the "Global North" with decolonizing epistemologies and narratives of the Anthropocene. Coining the term "genealogical liquefaction," he evaluates the contrasting ontologies of the Anthropocene by tracing their proposed colonial and cybernetic origin stories, identifying an epistemological rupture that confronts different ways of being in and of understanding the world. Drawing on Kathryn Yusoff, as well as on Sylvia Wynter and Walter Mignolo, Claus highlights a critical genealogy of the Anthropocene's colonial condition that actively unsettles the hegemonic Western discourse. Marie Heinrichs' contribution "NAVI/GATED/GAZE" also scrutinizes the hegemonic Western view of the world operated by "global players" such as Google. She argues that Google Earth's use of compiled satellite data embedded in computerized systems of representation and analysis such as geographic information systems (GIS) reinforce hegemonic power relations, and shows how these new technologies expand the territory on Earth and beyond to be colonized by state institutions and private companies. In questioning the appropriation processes of knowledge and territory in Western cartography, Heinrichs uncovers the problems behind Google's claim of environmental responsibility, and asks for less consuming and more self-reflective and critical practices of using mapping technologies.

Hannah Schmedes' article "A Laboratory for Living Off-World" contributes to this criticism by switching the focus away from human intention and action and adopting the perspective of "creepy crawlies," such as ants and cockroaches, in the Biosphere 2 enclosure, which prominently tested conditions for human settlements in space. In decentering the *anthropos*, she opts for a multispecies perspective on life on Earth and beyond. Finally, Petra Löffler's contribution "Colonizing the Ocean" follows in this critical evaluation of ecological colonialism by embracing the world-building and cohabiting capacity of corals. She advocates for the recognition of alternative modes of dealing with ecological catastrophes and the challenges of global warming and environmental degradation. In particular, her contribution criticizes the colonialism of Western knowledge production through the use of remote technologies to explore the deep sea and the establishment of underwater laboratories as test sites for space research.

All contributions offer critical geographical and epistemological explorations of the Anthropocene by tracing shifts in the ways that humans and non-humans, biotic and abiotic agents traverse, dwell in, and dream of space and place in tumultuous times. These longer essays are alternated with shorter interventions that offer a poetics for a harmed planet and the multiple worlds it contains. The essays and prose poems create a web of critical considerations and ideas about living and dying in the Anthropocene, a meshwork of many beginnings and loose endings, a diffractive reading of all the contradictions the Anthropocene brings about.

Towards a Critical Geography of the Anthropocene

Our volume highlights the entangled, interdependent nature of existence on Earth and beyond. Cascades of actions impact overlapping and intertwined human and non-human ecologies as plastic pollution, permacultures, and caring machines multiply on the same material planes. Examining detrimental anthropogenic ecological impact, as it proliferates through a capitalist-patriarchal-colonial development paradigm (Shiva 1988), requires an awareness of the global yet unequal distribution of the troubles brought forth by the Anthropocene. It requires a geo-ontological shift that is non-anthropocentric and conceptualizes the "human" both empathically and as a geological force (Zalasiewicz et al. 2019). Moreover, it requires researchers to critically orient themselves towards the world, to be aware of their standpoint (Harding 1991) and their situatedness (Haraway 1988) in social and epistemological relations, as well as in spatial structures. It requires, then, a geography that is aware of its racist-colonial implications (Yusoff 2018; Jazeel 2019). In the following section, we will walk the reader through not one single spatial turn, but rather a winding path or an epistemic zigzag between numerous disciplines in order to show how all of them build our volume's critical foundation.

Critical geographical scholarship is especially useful for our volume because it combines social theory, and specifically postcolonial and decolonial theory, with geographical investigations and allows a focus on both macro- and micro-scale topographical concerns. Entering into these conversations across disciplines and scales allows the contributors of this volume to investigate environmental degradations and extinctions as they unfold in places as small as the Biosphere 2 enclosure and as big as the nuclear testing sites of the Pacific, all the while helping them to explore unstable grounds such as river deltas or flooded areas.

Until the 1960s, geography was understood as a scientific discipline concerned with understanding the topographies of landscapes as both naturally developed and as influenced by human activities, but these analyses were largely disconnected from questions of social justice. The worldwide social movements of the 1960s led numerous geographers to depart from previously dominating quantitative methods and start incorporating social theory into their geographical inquiries (Smith 2001). Critical geographical scholarship of the time mainly incorporated a Marxist theoretical lens, later followed by feminist, post-colonial, and queer geographies, as well as geographies of disability. From the 1970s onwards, the humanities and social sciences also underwent a paradigm shift, which has come to be designated as the "spatial turn." Influenced by postmodernism, post-structuralism and deconstruction, this shift refuses the Cartesian concept of space as a simple container and asserts a relational concept of space "that takes into account other processes and phenomena, and in particular interactions of scale" (Torre 2008, 3).

Geographer David Harvey's monograph *Social Justice and the City* ([1973] 2009) devised a social theory for understanding structures of capital and class in urban areas and became a landmark text for critical geography. Moreover, Doreen Massey's *Space, Place, and Gender* (1994) provided a critical intervention to the field by bringing attention to how identities and mobilities shape both space itself and relations of power within it. In her landmark intervention *Feminism and Geography* (1993), Gillian Rose argues that feminist perspectives have been systematically sidelined in mainstream geographical analyses. In *Demonic Grounds* (2006), Katherine McKittrick locates Black women's historic negotiations of space and place in the diaspora in micro-landscapes such as slave auctions blocks and garrets, as well as in the macro-landscape of Canada—allowing her to highlight the land and country as they are produced by, and in co-productive relations with, race. Building on McKittrick, Tiffany Lethabo King (2019) unveils how Black fugitivity and Indigenous resistance presented a crisis for white settler geography by undermining its endeavors to depict a linear story of colonial conquest and stable boundaries. Our volume dwells on these positions of critical geography, as they provide tactical knowledge about the interdependencies of class, race, and gender with the production, colonization, and government of space.

As human geographer Tariq Jazeel (2019) points out, colonialism itself is an inherently geographic undertaking and postcolonialism is, despite originating in literary studies, concerned with the spatially differentiated effects of colonialism. Jazeel traces the emergence of a *postcolonial geography*, that is, geography genuinely influenced by the works of postcolonial theorists such as Edward Said and Homi K. Bhaba, to argue for a postcolonial methodology that takes the politics of representation and subjectivation as well as geography's various materialities into account "to develop critical postcolonial imaginations" (2019, 220). In the face of the Anthropocene, the task for postcolonial geography is to reveal the connections between histories of colonialism and histories of geology implicated in the life and death of non-humans. Similarly, Kathryn Yusoff's (2018) decolonial approach toward an Inhuman Geography stresses the inherent contradictions of the Anthropocene as a master narrative of modern science and criticizes its preoccupation with white supremacy and Western knowledge practices.

We must not forget that colonial-exploitative power relations are also happening at an extra-planetary scale. As historian Michael Rawson points out, the Copernican Revolution lifted extraterrestrial environments into the framework of environmental history (2015, 207), and this expansion of "nature" to other planets effectively rendered them exploitable. The emergence of systems ecology in the twentieth century, and most notably the popularization of James Lovelock and Lynn Margulis' Gaia Hypothesis ([1973] 2016), which transformed the understanding of the Earth into that of a self-regulating, complex system, coupled with the concurrent advancements in space technologies, have brought forth the hope of colonizing outer space by engineering closed systems elsewhere in the solar system (Anker, 2005; Höhler 2017). With the recent establishment of private companies—such as Virgin Galactic, SpaceX, and Blue Origin—that advocate for the colonization of outer space and the mining of asteroids as well as moons, the very materiality of outer space is becoming a space for colonial-capitalist settlement and exploitation. Space and place thus continue to be constructed, deconstructed, and otherwise negotiated both on Earth and beyond.

A critical geography of the Anthropocene, however, has the responsibility to go even further and break up the surface of these topographies to reveal other possible stratas of knowledge production and circulation. Stratigraphy therefore informs this volume on both a practical and a figurative level. According to feminist scholar Donna J. Haraway, figurations "are performative images that can be inhabited" and "can be condensed maps of contestable worlds" (1997, 11). Notions of sediments, depths, geologic layers or geographical longitudes and latitudes are therefore here considered not only as Western scientific concepts or models, but as figurations that have the ability to abstract maps and shape the narrated world dealt with in different realms of practice.

In their book *A Thousand Plateaus*, theorists Gilles Deleuze and Félix Guattari claim that stratification takes place *between* two strata, thus being a double-sided operation of assembling an *interstratum* and a *metastratum* at the same time (1987, 40). With the figuration of a "double articulation," they explain how connections and successions between material components are formed to build stable structures by "the process of 'sedimentation,' which deposits units of cyclic sediment" followed by a "'folding' that sets up a functional structure and affects the passage from sediment to sedimentary rock" (1987, 41). For Deleuze and Guattari, the sedimentation of formed matter indicates territorialities as well as "degrees of territorialization and deterritorialization" (1987, 41). Thus, stratigraphy in our volume acts as geological knowledge that reveals the power of both occupying and deranging a territory that is inherently political. In line with this thinking of stratigraphy, in his contribution Jakob Claus conceptualizes the figuration of liquefaction both as a geological and as an epistemological force able to unveil the interdependency between Western scientific and colonial practices. Moreover, as Petra Löffler shows in her contribution, Western scientists have considered even the liquid realm of the ocean as a stratified or—in Deleuze and Guattari's term—striated space to be explored and governed.

Media of Mapping

Media plays a crucial role in the dissemination of geographic knowledge. Understanding how maps shape formations of knowledge requires more than analyzing their contents and focusing on their very materialities. It requires us to relate the concept of mapped territory to representational techniques and power relations (Siegert 2011). Moreover, it is necessary to analyze these methods and power relations without restricting agency to human actors alone. In analyzing Galileo's telescopic observations of the moon, cultural theorist Joseph Vogl claims the "telescope is not just an extension of the senses," rather, it "creates the senses anew" (2007, 17). Thus, the telescope is attributed the agency to create and shape new worldviews. As sociologist of science Janet Vertesi shows in *Seeing like a Rover* (2015), these observations are far from bearing only historic relevance. The scientific image production of NASA's Mars Exploration Rover team is mediated through techno-scientific instruments at numerous stages of their work, which influences how visual data gathered through the rover are drawn onto maps. The capture and interpretation of these images requires the scientists to navigate the rover around the surface. Members of the team also openly describe their geological maps as "a sort of X-ray vision version of the landscape in which everything is colored according to your hypothesis" (110). Modelling of data to create maps, then, is inherently recursive: it not only encodes the worldviews of its creator but also generates these worldviews anew.

This line of inquiry will be taken up in Marie Heinrichs' contribution "NAVI/GATED/GAZE," which analyzes Google Earth's mobilization of the Whole Earth image as a political practice that uses the rhetoric of progressive environmentalism to capture market value. Heinrichs argues that Google Earth's algorithmically guided "gaze from nowhere" obfuscates the conditions and experiences of living in a world affected by anthropogenic climate change, while it simultaneously serves to centralize power in and accumulate capital for the company. Similarly, Petra Löffler's analysis of the extractive politics of colonial knowledge production shows how the development of sounding technologies and optical devices such as underwater cameras established a mediated gaze on the marine environment. This technologically enhanced view of the ocean explicitly led to the increased exploitation of the seabed as it drove scientists to collect, analyze, store, and display pieces of corals and other marine wildlife in museums while allowing mining companies to explore the deep sea with the help of submarine laboratories and rovers.

These contributions demonstrate how media as mediated infrastructures shape the world human observers are able to approach and thus create a world of their own. Geologist Peter K. Haff refers to these media infrastructures as a "technosphere." Haff regards technology itself as a global "geological phenomenon" (2013) that autonomously metabolizes fossil fuels and other energy resources similar to geological processes in the hydrosphere, lithosphere, atmosphere, or biosphere. In his conception of the technosphere, humans are only subcomponents necessary for maintaining the metabolism of the circulation of matter, energy, and information. But, as Haff also clarifies, the technosphere has not yet established a recycling mechanism, which is necessary for its longevity. Metals and raw materials have to be recycled to maintain the metabolic functionality of these technological systems and to guarantee that the technosphere can further evolve. Continued carbon emission without recycling would lead to severe systemic limitations and finally to a breakdown—which here includes the extinction of humans as well. From a geological point of view, the media infrastructures of the technosphere are circulating matter, energy and information "for its own uses" (Haff 2013, 307) —but not without the development of sustainable recycling mechanisms. Moreover, as Hannah Schmedes' contribution shows, the technosphere is challenged by non-human agencies such as ants and cockroaches that follow their own pursuits. Following Haff's postulates, we are convinced that there can only be sustainable futures for technology beyond the logics of colonialism, the logistics of capitalist extractionism, and the politics of environmental injustice and economic inequality between the "Global North" and the "Global South."

Ecologies Beyond Wilderness and Wasteland

Cultural theorist Raymond Williams famously wrote that "nature is perhaps the most complex word in the language" (2015, 164). Looking at scholarship, we already see this complexity as we encounter numerous terms denoting similar yet not identical concepts—landscape, Land, environment, habitat, wilderness and, for proponents of planetary scales, even Earth. Historian of science Peter Galison posits that the relationship between wilderness and wasteland is much more complicated and strange than a simple dichotomy. Because they are discursively formed as "twin zones of exclusion," places such as Chernobyl and the Nevada Test Site zones evoke conjoined categorizations of purity and defilement (Kruse and Galison 2011). The concept of the Anthropocene as it is enfolded across different disciplines as a boundary object is related to all of these terms in many ways. First, it resonates the mystified conception of an Edenic "pure" and passive nature, ready to be exploited and dominated. Second, it perpetuates the dialectics and dynamics of inclusion and exclusion even further: the Anthropocene is tied to geopolitical power relations that intensify social injustices such as racism with an unequal distribution of resources on the one hand and species extinctions on the other.

At the center of criticizing the Anthropocene, and more precisely the proposed unprecedented human influence on nature, lies the question of what elements are considered to reside within, and which elements are considered external to the notion of this "nature." Anthropologist Mary Douglas' 1966 influential study of the semiotics of pollution in *Purity and Danger* demonstrates that properties such as dirt and pollution have historically been regarded as "matter out of place," (36) and "rejected elements of ordered systems" (37)—no other knowledge formation makes this distinction more apparent than the discourse surrounding nature. The conception of nature as an outside, as that which is untouched by human efforts, has undergirded societal perceptions of the environment for centuries, and has subsequently been deployed both by environmentalists and industrialists for their respective ends. Environmental historian William Cronon's landmark article "The Trouble with Wilderness" (1996) explicitly criticizes such a purist understanding of the natural environment. Cronon argues that nature as a place to which to escape, to go back to one's roots, to find God, is not only a religious-nationalist construct based in ascribing sublime and frontier qualities to nature, but is also an inherently white, middle-class notion that further reproduces the subject's alienation from nature.

Far from the Euro-Western understanding that considers humans and nature separate, in Indigenous cosmologies, place and Land are considered intelligent and animate, "full of thought, desire, contemplation and will" (Watts 2013, 23); and they are regarded as the source and context for knowledge (Simpson 2014, 10). This fosters a strong and intimate connection between Indigenous peoples and the Land and strengthens the understanding of interdependence between their existences. Through the lens of Western philosophy cultural theorist Levi R. Bryant (2013) likewise critiques the prevailing narrative of culture residing outside of nature, bringing forward the faulty understanding that ecology matters only to those who wish to aid conservation efforts, and ultimately states that culture has to be understood *as* nature. He conceptualizes ecology as an inquiry into *relations and interactions* not solely between organic entities, but also physical media and the material implications of discursive formations.

As environmental humanities scholar Shannon Cram shows, the material-discursive mediation between uncontaminated and contaminated areas has also been utilized in service of the nuclear industry, where plants and animals become "proof of post-nuclear perseverance" (Cram 2016, 95). Radioactive ecologies thus serve as evidence of survival rather than destruction. The categorizations of landscapes and the concept of purity are central considerations in our volume because they shed light on the politics and dynamics of exclusion and inclusion that are crucial for assembling a critical atlas of the Anthropocene. Tómas Uzón shows in his contribution that the conquest over a territory is organized along the difference between destruction and preservation. In a similar vein, Petra Löffler's piece discusses the nuclear test site on Bikini Atoll as a contested space: a laboratory for "radiation ecology" that has become a "debrisphere," and at the same time a site of Indigenous resistance to reclaim ownership of their expropriated land. As these examples show, the relation between wilderness and wasteland is complex and always governed by geopolitical power relations.

Agencies of Human and Non-Human Entities

The last decades have seen the emergence of a series of movements across disciplines that contest anthropocentrism, challenge traditional notions of subjectivity by assigning agency to non-humans, and examine discordant relations between material processes and cultural practices (Connolly 2013, 399). Such movements are most commonly referred to as "New Materialism," a term coined by philosophers Manuel DeLanda and Rosi Braidotti towards the end of the 1990s (Dolphijn and Tuin 2012, 48). Feminist theorist Karen Barad's *Meeting the Universe Halfway* (2007), and in particular her advancement of the theory of agential realism, has been foundational for the field. Based on insights from quantum physics and Judith Butler's feminist materialism, Barad demonstrates how matter is always in the making and bears an agency of its own. Her thinking of "intra-activity" and her methodology of diffraction offer profound perspectives on the processuality and material-discursive relatedness of all kinds and forms of always entangled matter. Feminist scholars in the field have developed a material ethics focusing on practices as always "embodied, situated actions" (Alaimo and Hekman 2008, 7). Following this perspective, in *Vibrant Matter* (2010) political theorist Jane Bennett argues that political theory too ought to consider matter as possessing agency.

Regardless, even within this scholarly move away from human-centered inquiries, human exceptionalism is hard to shake: as Susan Leigh Star points out, the syntactical anthropocentrism of the non-human remains, as the designation itself "implies a lack of something" (quoted in Kirksey and Helmreich 2010, 555). In her influential monograph *Geontologies* (2016), anthropologist Elizabeth A. Povinelli coined the term "geontopower" to center the manifold power structures inherent to the differentiation between *bios* and *geos*, the living and the non-living. In her exploration of the numerous manifestations of this mode of governance of late liberal capitalism employed by the carbon liberation imaginary, Povinelli engages questions of extinction and sustainability from a multispecies point of view.

Importantly, as feminist science studies scholar Juno Salazar Parreñas' *Decolonizing Extinction* (2018) has shown, recognizing the agential power of non-humans and acknowledging the destructive capacity of humans on the environment does not necessarily translate to the cultivation of non-violent relations. Her findings show that even though conservation practices are presented as stemming from a *benevolent* desire to repair disturbed ecologies, their onto-epistemological scaffolding is rooted in anthropocentric control fantasies that inherently inflict violence on the species that it aims to help "conserve" (Salazar Parreñas 2018, 84). In a move to further complicate the understanding of the ethical implications of non-human agencies, media scholar Sy Taffel argues that entangled intra-active histories of plastic and media, coupled with contemporary throwaway culture, implicates plastics in the ecological systems of oceans in particular, and he contends that oceanic plastics function both as destructive *and* productive agents. As destructive agents, plastics affect the agential capacities of marine wildlife by, for example, leaving species unable to breath or nourish themselves due to ingesting plastic. As productive agents, however, oceanic plastics have fostered the development of certain types of microorganisms that reside inside and feed on it.

Thinking through trajectories that unsettle a preoccupation with singularly human agency and survival allows the authors of this volume to contextualize the world-ending and world-building powers of environmental collapse through pluralized subjects. Hannah Schmedes' reframing of the Biosphere 2 experiment through the perspective of cockroaches and ants sheds light on how situations of collapse and failure for some beings can generate systems of abundance and success for others. In doing so, Schmedes' piece pushes towards significant teleological and axiological shifts in thinking regarding the value and "purpose" of nature as well as the place of humans and non-humans within it. Petra Löffler's contribution contrasts the world-building and repairing ecological power of corals with their history in the natural sciences, ultimately revealing the enduring ties of the natural sciences to colonial politics and extractive practices.

It is important to remember that the New Materialist revisions to agential relations have drawn numerous decolonial critiques, particularly due to their turning of a blind eye towards many Indigenous epistemologies to which relationality and material agency are foundational (Tallbear 2017). As Chinese-Métis artist Sebastian De Line explains, the philosophical stance that all matter is animate and interconnected – also known as *Niw_hk_m_kanak*, which he translates as "all my/our relations" – is in fact "a basis for science, law and philosophy within Indigenous cultures" (2016). Other anti-colonial thinkers remind us that the human-non-human distinction is also troubled by the exclusionary function of humanness and the category human. As Sylvia Wynter argues, the "invention of Man" was only made possible through the invention of the concept of "race" and "colonizer/colonized relations," which cast Black and brown people as inherently "racially inferior," and continuously assimilated all dark-skinned peoples into the category of the Other (2003, 266). In her analysis of the emergence of geology and the language of the Anthropocene through Wynter's scholarship, Kathryn Yusoff suggests that agency, matter, and race are all intimately connected, where "the border in the division of materiality (and its subjects) as inhuman and human, and thus as inert or agentic matter, operationalizes race" (2018, 4). Thinking with these feminist scholars allows Jakob Claus, in his contribution, to trace the fractures and frictions of the Anthropocene discourse.

Questions of unsettling agency in the Anthropocene discourse therefore have to start with the simultaneous recognition that ontologies operating outside of human exceptionalism have existed and continue to exist under settler-colonial domination, as well as the understanding that it is exactly settler-colonial, or colonizer/colonizer, relations that have reinforced the superiority and singular agency of a Western *anthropos*—which has not only semantically, but also materially, shaped our current geological epoch. In striving toward understanding diversified multispecies perspectives on entangled material environments, we also note the importance of decolonizing practices that recognize Indigenous knowledges and stand in solidarity against settler colonial forces and structures (Tuck and Yang 2012).

Beyond the Anthropocene(s)

As a scientific concept, the Anthropocene has come to denote the claim that because humans have come to exert global influence over the Earth's ecosystems, the geological epoch of the Holocene has been superseded by a human-dominated period in the history of Earth. Yet neither the International Commission on Stratigraphy (ICS) nor the International Union of Geological Sciences has formally accepted the term as a new category of geological time. The possible beginnings of the new geological epoch are widely debated, both among geologists and in the humanities, and the various proposed epochal turning points range all the way from the Neolithic Revolution through the beginning of colonization to the peak in radionuclide fallout resulting from atomic bomb testing during the 1950s (Zalasiewicz et al. 2019, chap. 7; Davis and Todd 2017; Yusoff 2018, 23–24). Historian George Holmes points out that the commencing date of the Anthropocene has high ethical stakes for debates in biodiversity conservation, as the date could challenge conceptions of "the naturalness of many ecosystems and baselines for ecological restorations" (2015, 89). As the previous sections have highlighted, the shifts in scholarly thinking regarding space, time, nature, and technology, as well as agency, all contribute to how current scholarly, scientific, and artistic debates surrounding the Anthropocene are developing. As a boundary object, however, the Anthropocene changes from where and *when* you are standing – and the lens through which you are looking (Horn and Bergthaler 2020).

Understanding the *temporal* scale of the stratigraphic and topographic impacts of humans on the "environment" is central to a critical geography of the Anthropocene. It is not only a question of beginnings, or what the start date of such an epoch should be, but also of what living and non-living assemblages this new geological epoch evolves. And it is the question of an end, or what can be understood as the Anthropocene as a crisis narrative: the question of how much time there is still left of the world as "we" know it. In his influential article "The Climate of History: Four Theses" (2009), historian Dipesh Chakrabarty traces the shift from understanding humanity as a biological agent to a universalized geological force arguing that this has resulted in the collapse of the distinction between human and natural histories. He calls for a new concept of historicity beyond the "deep time" of geology and the natural sciences. This collapsing of time, of natural and human history centers the question of agency in the Anthropocene.

In *After Finitude* (2008), philosopher Quentin Meillassoux investigates the rational methods of geologists and archaeologists to date material objects that are older than any intelligent life on Earth, terming such materials *arche-fossils* because of their ability, in the eyes of Western scientists, to make possible statements about an ancestral world. According to Meillassoux this Western rationality implies a retrojection of the past from the present givenness of *arche-fossils*. Analyzing the contradictions in Western rational philosophy and natural sciences he opts for an understanding of ancestrality and time without a human observer or a technical quantification of time. This "othering" of time is essential for our volume insofar as it makes it conceivable to imagine other worlds of multi-species entanglements beyond humans, and, possibly, even beyond life on Earth.

The question of time in the Anthropocene is not simply a question of the dating of a singular event or of a whole epoch in the first place, but also a question of pacing. Due to the enormous timescales that the formation of combustible geologic deposits such as oil, coal, and gas require in contrast to the relatively short period it is taking for anthropogenic forces to exploit them, time plays a role in the uneven adaptation of non-human systems to human-wrought activities. A large number of organisms and ecosystems are unable to adjust, "to keep pace" with anthropogenic ecological changes. Taffel argues that "ecological crises are thus understood not as enacting (cultural) change to an otherwise static (natural) system but as increasing the pace of change within dynamic ecosystems beyond the adaptive potential of numerous biotic actors" (2019, 366). Given the fact that capitalism organizes economic, social and ecological relations as well, it then requires both humans and non-humans to recalibrate to the hegemonic time in order to fulfill its own demands. And just as not all humans are able to adjust their time to the demands of the dominant social classes, some non-humans are unable to adapt to these temporal pressures as well. The inability or unwillingness to adapt to a certain environment thus becomes a force of resistance against the logics and logistics of late or neoliberal capitalism. From this perspective, the Anthropocene, which McKenzie Wark has designated as a "slow-motion emergency" (2015), can more accurately be understood as one that is not-quite-slow-enough.

Temporal phenomena such as pace, speed, acceleration, and rhythm are materially related with spatial phenomena such as landscapes, habitats, or ecosystems. The one is not prior to the other. Complexities emerge from their interrelatedness—or they are reduced when relations between material entities break down. This is what Karan Barad means by *spacetime-mattering* (2007). This is also why figurations of flux such as the fluvial landscapes of river deltas play a crucial role in criticism of the geological foundation of the Anthropocene. Questions of temporal scale and questions of agency are therefore insep-arably tethered. Jörg Dünne's piece in our volume highlights contemporary Argentinian literature's contestation of human and geologic timescales and the agential power of non-human agents. His examples include literary works that focus on alluvium as a formational agent of the river delta, as well as ones that unsettle the hegemonic understanding of agency by insisting that world-building agency is not wielded by matter alone, but rather by the *unity* of matter and time.

Advocating for partial, plural perspectives also means grappling with the fact that futures might evolve *beyond* the existence of the human species. If complexity can be seen as an "adaptation to specific ecological conditions" (Hejnol 2017, 96) figuring a coral-like rhizomatic meshwork of entangled species, then life is inherently complex at every stage. When Donna J. Haraway (2016) claims that humans are humus, what she highlights is the fact that life reorganizes itself in plurifying ways across the boundaries of life and non-life. Through such a cosmological lens, all material entities are entangled through enormous timescales and spaces in a *pluriverse* (James 1909, de la Cadena and Blaser 2018), not a universe. As numerous scholars have shown, creating a just future, a future beyond the Anthropocene that is attuned to the needs of multi-species material entanglements, starts from the very recognition of the radical complexity of being (Escobar 2018, Kothari et al. 2019). This is exactly the conversation that our volume aims to contribute to: the unsettling of hegemonic monist epistemologies through the acknowledgment of the infinitely complex entanglements that existing and dwelling in diverse spaces and times entail. It is for this reason that we invite our readers to walk the flexible "caucho path" with us, as it has been envisioned by Mátyás Sirokai: to provide us with "not power but momentum, [to] desire not what's been but what's to come."

Berlin and Toronto, summer 2020

We are grateful to the sponsors: Humboldt-Universitäts-Gesellschaft, the Canadian Embassy, Humboldt Labor, and the Faculty of Humanities and Social Sciences, as well as the Institute of Cultural History and Theory at Humboldt University of Berlin, especially Holger Brohm, Christine Schneider, Yvonne Kult, and Simone Damis, without whose continuous support the "Atlas of the Anthropocene" symposium could not have taken place. Hearty thanks to all the presenters at the conference for their genuine and generous intellectual engagement with each other's ideas. A special thanks to the xtro realm group for allowing the reprint of the prose poems included in their transmedial extrodæsia encyclopedia. We are also thankful for the conversations with Reed McConnell that have sparked the idea for the symposium, as well as for her help in organizing it. The volume profited from conversations with many colleagues and friends: Sabine Höhler, Änne Söll, Florian Sprenger, Rebecca Woods, Lindsay LeBlanc, Salina Suri, Nelanthi Hewa, and R. Blair Frost gave invaluable advice at several stages. We also thank our publisher meson press, namely Marcus Burkhardt and Andreas Kirchner, who have been enthusiastic about the project from the start. Last but not least, we are thankful for the cover design by Claudia Mareis.

References

Alaimo, Stacy, and Susan Hekman. 2008. *Material Feminisms*. Bloomington: University of Indiana Press.

Anker, Peder. 2005. "The Ecological Colonization of Space." *Environmental History* 10 (2): 239–68.

Barad, Karen. 2007. *Meeting the Universe Halfway: Quantum Physics and the Entanglement of Matter and Meaning*. Durham, NC: Duke University Press.

Bennett, Jane. 2010. *Vibrant Matter: A Political Ecology of Things*. Durham, NC: Duke University Press.

Bonneuil, Christophe, and Jean-Baptiste Fressoz. 2016. *The Shock of the Anthropocene: The Earth, History and Us*. New York: Verso Books.

Bryant, Levi R. 2013. "Black." In *Prismatic Ecology: Ecotheory beyond Green*, edited by Jeffrey Jerome Cohen, 290–310. Minneapolis: University of Minnesota Press.

Chakrabarty, Dipesh. 2009. "The Climate of History: Four Theses." *Critical Inquiry* 35 (2): 197–222. https://doi.org/10.1086/596640.

Connolly, William E. 2013. "The 'New Materialism' and the Fragility of Things." *Millennium: Journal of International Studies* 41 (3): 399–412. https://doi.org/10.1177/0305829813486849.

Cram, Shannon. 2016. "Wild and Scenic Wasteland: Conservation Politics in the Nuclear Wilderness." *Environmental Humanities* 7 (1): 89–105. https://doi.org/10.1215/22011919-3616344.

Cronon, William. 1996. "The Trouble with Wilderness: Or, Getting Back to the Wrong Nature." *Environmental History* 1 (1): 7–28. https://doi.org/10.2307/3985059.

Crutzen, Paul J., and Eugene F. Stoermer. 2000. "The 'Anthropocene.'" *IGBP Newsletter* 41 (May): 17–18.

Davis, Heather, and Zoe Todd. 2017. "On the Importance of a Date, or, Decolonizing the Anthropocene." *ACME: An International Journal for Critical Geographies* 16 (4): 761–80.

de la Cadena, Marisol, and Mario Blaser. 2018. *A World of Many Worlds*. Durham, NC: Duke University Press.

De Line, Sebastian. 2016. "All My / Our Relations: Can Posthumanism Be Decolonized?" *Open!* July 7. Accessed January 16, 2021. https://onlineopen.org/all-my-our-relations.

Deleuze, Gilles, and Guattari, Félix. 1987. *A Thousand Plateaus: Capitalism and Schizophrenia*. Translated by Brian Massumi. Minneapolis: University of Minnesota Press.

Didi-Huberman, Georges. 2018. *Atlas, Or the Anxious Gay Science: How to Carry the World on One's Back?* Chicago/London: University of Chicago Press.

Dolphijn, Rick, and Iris van der Tuin. 2012. *New Materialism: Interviews & Cartographies*. Ann Arbor: Open Humanities Press.

Douglas, Mary. (1966) 2005. *Purity and Danger: An Analysis of the Concepts of Pollution and Taboo*. Reprint, London: Routledge.

Escobar, Arturo. 2018. *Designs for the Pluriverse: Radical Interdependence, Autonomy, and the Making of Worlds*. Durham, NC: Duke University Press.

Guattari, Félix. 1992. *Chaosmosis: An Ethico-aesthetic Paradigm*. Translated by Paul Bains and Julian Prefanis. Bloomington: Indiana University Press.

Haff, Peter K. 2013. "Technology as a Geological Phenomenon: Implications for Human Well-being." In *A Stratigraphical Basis for the Anthropocene*, edited by C. N. Waters, J. A. Zalasiewicz, M. Williams, M. A. Ellis, and A. M. Snelling, 301–9. London: Geological Society, Special Publications.

Hall, Stuart, and Bram Gieben, eds. (1992) 2011. *Formations of Modernity*. Understanding Modern Societies 1. Cambridge: Polity Press.

Haraway, Donna J. 1988. "Situated Knowledges: The Science Question in Feminism and the Privilege of Partial Perspective." *Feminist Studies* 14 (3): 575–99. https://doi.org/10.2307/3178066.

Haraway, Donna J. 1997. *Modest_Witness@Second Millenium. FemaleMan©_Meets_OncoMouse™. Feminisms and Technoscience*. New York: Routledge.

Haraway, Donna J. 2015. "Anthropocene, Capitalocene, Plantationocene, Chthulucene: Making Kin." *Environmental Humanities* 6: 159–65.

Haraway, Donna J. 2016. *Staying with the Trouble: Making Kin in the Chthulucene.* Durham, NC: Duke University Press.

Harding, Sandra G. 1991. *Whose Science? Whose Knowledge? Thinking from Women's Lives.* Ithaca, NY: Cornell University Press.

Harvey, David. (1973) 2009. *Social Justice and the City.* Revised edition. Athens, GA: University of Georgia Press.

Hejnol, Andreas. 2017. "Ladders, Trees, Complexity, and other Metaphors in Evolutionary Thinking." In *Arts of Living on a Damaged Planet: Ghosts and Monsters of the Anthropocene,* edited by Anna Tsing, Heather Swanson, Elaine Gan, and Nils Bubandt, 87–102. Minneapolis: University of Minnesota Press.

Hessler, Stefanie. 2020. "Rising Tides." In *Down to Earth: Klima – Kunst – Diskurs Unplugged*, 89–103. Berlin: medialis.

Höhler, Sabine. 2017. "Survival: Mars Fiction and Experiments with Life on Earth." *Environmental Philosophy* 14 (1): 83–100. https://doi.org/10.5840/envirophil201731646.

Holmes, George. 2015. "What Do We Talk About When We Talk About Biodiversity Conservation in the Anthropocene?" *Environment and Society* 6 (1): 87–108. https://doi.org/10.3167/ares.2015.060106.

Horn, Eva, and Hannes Bergthaler. 2020. *The Anthropocene: Key Issues for the Humanities.* London: Routledge.

James, William. 1909. *A Pluralistic Universe: Hibbert Lectures at Manchester College on the Present Situation in Philosophy.* New York: Longmans, Green.

Jazeel, Tariq. 2019. *Postcolonialism.* London: Routledge.

King, Tiffany Lethabo. 2019. *The Black Shoals: Offshore Formations of Black and Native Studies.* Durham, NC: Duke University Press.

Kirksey, S. Eben, and Stefan Helmreich. 2010. "The Emergence of Multispecies Ethnography." *Cultural Anthropology* 25 (4): 545–76. https://doi.org/10.1111/j.1548-1360.2010.01069.x.

Kruse, Jamie, and Peter Galison. 2011. "Waste-Wilderness: A Conversation with Peter L. Galison." *Friends of the Pleistocene* (blog). Accessed September 1, 2020. https://fopnews.wordpress.com/2011/03/31/galison/.

Kothari, Ashish, Ariel Salleh, Arturo Escobar, Federico Demaria, and Alberto Acosta, eds. 2019. *Pluriverse: A Post-Development Dictionary.* New Delhi: Tulika Books.

Lovelock, James, and Lynn Margulis. (1973) 2016. "Atmospheric Homeostasis by and for the Biosphere: The Gaia Hypothesis". *Tellus* 26 (1–2): 2–10. doi: 10.3402/tellusa.v26i1-2.9731.

Massey, Doreen. 1994. *Space, Place and Gender.* Cambridge: Polity Press.

McKittrick, Katherine. 2006. *Demonic Grounds: Black Women and the Cartographies of Struggle.* Minneapolis: University of Minnesota Press.

Meillassoux, Quentin. 2008. *After Finitude: An Essay on the Necessity of Contingency.* Introduction by Alain Badiou. London: Continuum.

Mignolo, Walter D. 2011. *The Darker Side of Western Modernity: Global Futures, Decolonial Options.* Durham, NC: Duke University Press.

Moore, Jason W. 2015. *Capitalism in the Web of Life: Ecology and the Accumulation of Capital*. London: Verso Books.

Pálsson, Gisli, Bronislaw Szerszynski, Sverker Sörlin, John Marks, Bernard Avril, Carole Crumley, Heide Hackmann, et al. 2013. "Reconceptualizing the 'Anthropos' in the Anthropocene: Integrating the Social Sciences and Humanities in Global Environmental Change Research." *Environmental Science & Policy*. Special Issue: Responding to the Challenges of our Unstable Earth (RESCUE). 28 (April): 3–13. https://doi.org/10.1016/j.envsci.2012.11.004.

Parreñas, Juno Salazar. 2018. *Decolonizing Extinction: The Work of Care in Orangutan Rehabilitation*. Durham, NC: Duke University Press.

Povinelli, Elizabeth A. 2016. *Geontologies: A Requiem to Late Liberalism*. Durham, NC: Duke University Press.

Puig de la Bellacasa, María. 2017. *Matters of Care: Speculative Ethics in More than Human Worlds*. Minneapolis: University of Minnesota Press.

Rabasa, José. 2006. "Allegories of Atlas." In *The Post-Colonial Studies Reader*, edited by Bill Ashcroft, Gareth Griffiths, and Helen Tiffin, 358–64. London: Routledge.

Rawson, M. 2015. "Discovering the Final Frontier: The Seventeenth-Century Encounter with the Lunar Environment." *Environmental History* 20 (2): 194–216. https://doi.org/10.1093/envhis/emv003.

Rose, Gillian. 1993. *Feminism and Geography: The Limits of Geographical Knowledge*. Cambridge: Polity Press.

Said, Edward. 1993. *Culture and Imperialism*. New York: Knopf.

Shiva, Vandana. 1988. *Staying Alive: Women, Ecology, and Survival in India*. New Delhi: Kali for Women.

Siegert, Bernhard. 2011. "The Map Is the Territory." *Radical Philosophy* (blog). Accessed March 21, 2020. www.radicalphilosophy.com/article/the-map-is-the-territory.

Simpson, Leanne Betasamosake. 2014. "Land as Pedagogy: Nishnaabeg Intelligence and Rebellious Transformation." *Decolonization: Indigeneity, Education & Society* 3 (3). https://jps.library.utoronto.ca/index.php/des/article/view/22170.

Smith, Neil. 2001. "Marxism and Geography in the Anglophone World." *Geographische Revue* 3 (1): 5–21.

Star, Susan Leigh, and James R. Griesemer. 1989. "Institutional Ecology, 'Translations' and Boundary Objects: Amateurs and Professionals in Berkeley's Museum of Vertebrate Zoology, 1907–39." *Social Studies of Science* 19 (3): 387–420.

Stengers, Isabelle. 2010. *Cosmopolitics*. Posthumanities 9–10. Minneapolis: University of Minnesota Press.

TallBear, Kim. 2017. "Beyond the Life/Not-Life Binary: A Feminist-Indigenous Reading of Cryopreservation, Interspecies Thinking, and the New Materialisms." In *Cryopolitics: Frozen Life in a Melting World*, edited by Joanna Radin and Emma Kowal, 179–202. Cambridge: MIT Press.

Taffel, Sy. 2019. *Digital Media Ecologies*. London: Bloomsbury Academic.

Torre, Angelo. 2008. "A 'Spatial Turn' in History? Landscapes, Visions, Resources." *Annales. Histoire, Sciences Sociales* 63 (5): 1127–44.

Tuck, Eve, and K. Wayne Yang. 2012. "Decolonization Is Not a Metaphor." *Decolonization: Indigeneity, Education & Society* 1 (1): 1–40. https://jps.library.utoronto.ca/index.php/des/article/view/18630.

Wark, McKenzie. 2015. *Molecular Red: Theory for the Anthropocene*. London: Verso.

Vertesi, Janet. 2015. *Seeing Like a Rover: How Robots, Teams, and Images Craft Knowledge of Mars*. Chicago: University of Chicago Press.

Vogl, Joseph. 2007. "Becoming-Media: Galileo's Telescope." *Grey Room* 29 (October): 14–25. https://doi.org/10.1162/grey.2007.1.29.14.

Watts, Vanessa. 2013. "Indigenous Place-Thought and Agency Amongst Humans and Non Humans (First Woman and Sky Woman Go On a European World Tour!)." *Decolonization: Indigeneity, Education & Society* 2 (1). https://jps.library.utoronto.ca/index.php/des/article/view/19145.

Williams, Raymond. 2014. *Keywords: A Vocabulary of Culture and Society*. Oxford: Oxford University Press.

Wynter, Sylvia. 2003. "Unsettling the Coloniality of Being/Power/Truth/Freedom: Towards the Human, After Man, Its Overrepresentation—An Argument." *CR: The New Centennial Review* 3 (3): 257–337. https://doi.org/10.1353/ncr.2004.0015.

Yusoff, Kathryn. 2018. *A Billion Black Anthropocenes or None*. Minneapolis: University of Minnesota Press.

Zalasiewicz, Jan, Colin N. Waters, Mark Williams and Colin P. Summerhayes. 2019. *The Anthropocene as a Geologic Time Unit: A Guide to the Scientific Evidence and Current Debate*. Cambridge: Cambridge University Press.

Plant-time

Kornélia Deres

Slow theatre. At a green tempo, meditatively.
Only epidermal cells could peel off quite
so discreetly. We're of the same species:
the oxygen and carbon dioxide are mere
supporting roles. The contained, corpulent
greens reach into the air, they cough it out.
Their coughs are sweet victuals. They've no
need for a greenhouse, they'll gobble it up
anyway, they'll bite through its scratches. No
need for respirators, for washing. They can
take it. When Noah embarked nature, he left
the trees behind because he didn't have the
time. Sight-specific revenge. The new ark is
being made of human bones and cerebral
cortices.

Translated by Owen Good

EARLY-WARNING SYSTEM

MITIGATION INFRASTRUCTURE

BOUNDARY OBJECTS

ONTOLOGICAL DISPUTES

GLACIAL LAKE OUTBURST FLOODS

[2]

Memory Regimes and the Anthropocene: Tracing Causes and Responsibilities under Flood Risk Scenarios in Ancash, Peru

Tomás J. Usón

The notion of the Anthropocene is shaped by diverse spatial and temporal scales. While this discussion settles several challenges for scholars and scientists, it also leads to intense debates on the causes and responsibilities of climatic transformations due to anthropogenic emissions. Notably, consideration of memory practices around climatic disasters may play an important role in reaching an agreement about the responsibility and liability of different parties when talking about anthropogenically-induced climate change. But it can also jeopardize the possibility of reaching a consensus, leading to irreconcilable positions between different world arrangements. In this article, I analyze two cases of flood controversies in the region of Ancash, Peru:

Lake 513 and Lake Palcacocha. Both lakes pose high risks to the population downstream due to possible glacial lake outburst floods (GLOF). The diverse set of actors affected, however, reduces the capacity to reach agreements about the causes and consequences of those threats. Building on the notions of boundary objects and ontological disputes, I reflect on how difficult it is for actors with diverse ontological backgrounds and world arrangements to achieve a consensus on political climate resolutions. The article concludes by stressing the relevance of relational arenas for the interaction of different projects of world production, even if this interaction does not always lead to mutual understanding.

The declaration of the Anthropocene as the current geological epoch has left substantial consequences for defining the temporal conditions for a planetary history. On the one hand, the anthropocentric regime requires expanding the temporal boundaries that we humans have been using for narrating our past so far. Equating the Anthropos to the erosive capacity of wind and water, or even to the destructive creation of volcanic eruptions and tectonic activity, means expanding the history of humankind and incorporating it into the history of geological processes. It is the ultimate assertion of the post-humanities: the recognition of humans, non-humans, or even other-than-humans, as equally central agents in what Bruno Latour (2017) has assertively named the "geostory"—the story of our common, but also divergent, worlds. Such recognition does not mean either a naturalization of humans nor a humanization of nature. It merely recognizes that the history, the narration of humankind in the world, is intrinsically related to the incommensurable forces, elements and agents of Gaia, that complex self-regulating system that James Lovelock and Lynn Margulis ([1973] 2016) described as the interaction among living and non-living agents constantly transforming the biosphere.[1]

The Anthropocene, on the other hand, also implies compressing the temporal range considered for geological epochs—together with the necessary time for geological transformations at a large scale—by incorporating a little fraction of the history of the Earth into the annals of the geostory. Processes of carbon concentration in the atmosphere that used to take millennia are now happening in the span of years. The last time that the CO_2 in the atmosphere hovered at the current levels—around 400 parts per million (ppm)—was during the Pliocene 2.5 million years ago. After the last big ice age around 12,000 years ago, and with the beginning of the Holocene, carbon concentration fluctuated between 260 and 285 ppm, with variations of less than 5ppm in the past millennium. In recent decades, CO_2 levels have been rising by 2ppm every year (Dlugokencky et al. 2019).

When the beginning of the geological and climatic capacity of humans and their technological apparatus took place, however, is still a matter of discussion (see Povinelli 2016). The same way as a magma chamber can take years, centuries, or even millennia, to accumulate the required amount of pressure for a volcanic eruption, the geological influence of humankind can be diverse depending on which development is considered to be the beginning of such influence. While some scholars emphasize the invention of agriculture and with it the first population boom during the Neolithic period 12,000 years ago, others like Paul

1 Gaia, according to Latour (2017), is more than a simple metaphor to understand the interconnections among entities in the planet. It is the self-regulated entity that mobilizes all actors, whether humans and other-than-humans, in the same geostory. To recognize the equal protagonists of all the entities within the Earth system is to recognize their agency, whose assemblage is delegated to—and coordinated by—Gaia.

 Crutzen and Eugene Stoermer (2000), who popularized the term Anthropocene, put their cards on the beginning of the Industrial Revolution in the eighteenth century. Authors like Timothy Morton (2013, 7) even go further by arguing that the end of the world took place when James Watt patented the steam engine in 1784—"an act that commenced the depositing of carbon in Earth's crust (…) and the inception of humanity as a geophysical force on a planetary scale." Some scientists stress that the detonations of atomic bombs in 1945 by the US army—first as part of the Trinity Test in New Mexico and later with the nuclear bombing in Hiroshima and Nagasaki—and the progression of nuclear tests in the Pacific in the following decades showed us that the Earth was something that could eventually be destroyed by human action (Zalasiewicz et al. 2015).

Discussions on the inauguration of the Anthropocene make one thing clear: the boundaries between this epoch and its predecessor, the Holocene, are not clearly discernible. These disagreements over defining the inaugural event of the Anthropocene have little to do with scientific inconsistency. It is mostly a matter of narrative, and how the different disciplines have agreed on temporal standards for its definition. The Anthropocene is much more than the liberation of massive amounts of CO_2 into the atmosphere and the polluting of the earth and the sea. It is the foundation of one of the most decisive philosophical, anthropological, political, and even religious epochs of human history (Latour 2017)—a definition that is intrinsically influenced by how the existence of humankind and its interconnections with its environment are narrated and acted out in the present. If we assume the Anthropocene is an epoch of multiple narratives and geopolitical interests, where humans and man-made technologies are meant to have different impacts on the Earth, would not this also imply the assumption of an era with multiple temporalities and localities? Should it not be better to talk about a geological period of time with several beginnings and, eventually, endings?

In what follows, I explore these questions by analyzing how different narrations of the past might lead to—apparently—irreconcilable understandings of climatic disasters, and how we can deal with such differences without neglecting them. First, the article expounds some theoretical discussions regarding the notion of memory regimes, and how these could help us to explore discussions on causes and responsibilities in times of the Anthropocene. This accomplished, I present two cases of climate controversy in Ancash, Peru: those of Lake 513 and Lake Palcacocha, using them to exemplify the divergences that heterogenous explanations of climatic events might entail. These cases are analyzed based on the findings of ethnographic fieldwork I conducted from November 2019 to March 2020 in the region, which included in-depth interviews with local actors, participant observation, and document analysis. Building on the notions of boundary objects and ontological disputes, the article concludes by recognizing the Anthropocene as an arena of discrepancies—an invitation for overcoming the idea of a unified world with a homogeneous past.

Narrating the Anthropocene: Setting the Boundaries

Questions about the narratives of the Anthropocene—and the standards used for its delimitation—lead us to a highly relevant topic: the way that past events are coherently presented in forms of memory practices. Memory, as the French philosopher Henri Bergson (1911) famously argued, involves a dynamic process of transmission and transformation rather than a repository of lineally unfolded history from past to present. The practice of remembering implies the actualization of the "unlimited experience" (Bergson 1911, 186) of the past. It is the reduction of the virtual, that passive potentiality that no longer acts, into the limited conditions of the present—the "actual." The actual, at the same time, is in a constant process of virtualization as the present is preserved in duration or, as Middleton and Brown (2005, 62) put it, "the experience of time passing." This continual process of actualization and virtualization is what memory involves—"the action of committing record, to leave invisible traces verifying the veracity of an event," according to Geoffrey Bowker (2005, 7).

One of Bergson's most fascinating contributions to the studies on memory is the object-oriented approach he proposes. For the author, remembering is not an abstract act of "storing" that takes place in people's minds. It is instead a process mediated by materiality that provides the proper conditions for the reconstruction of the past. The double process of virtualization and actualization requires concrete objects containing traces of duration, giving non-human actors a central role in practices of memory.[2] In the case of disaster memory, materiality does not just include representations *per se* of disasters, such as paintings, photographs, film footages, books, and newspapers (Juneja and Schenk 2014; Agostinho 2015); it also considers traces like flood marks, which "work to blur distinctions between the past and present and to condense the different events in time, which they originally referred to, within a perception of disaster as a single repetitive event" (Juneja and Schenk 2014, 9).

Although memory is commonly associated with the collective efforts of civil society, scientific and planning reasoning are also producers of their own practices of memory, whether explicitly or implicitly. Scientific studies look for traces of previous events to materialize their magnitudes and impacts into models, maps, and diagrams used for the politics of preparedness and

2 Further approaches, such as Actor-Network Theory (ANT), have explored this mediating condition of objects through the notion of translation, namely, "all the negotiations, intrigues, calculations, acts of persuasion and violence, thanks to which an actor [whether human or non-human] or force takes, or causes to be conferred on itself, authority to speak or act on behalf of another actor or force" (Callon and Latour 1981, 279). For a deeper analysis about the notion of translation and memory, see Middleton and Brown (2005, 145–57).

recovery, including master and regulatory plans articulating urban environments (November, Camacho-Hübner, and Latour 2010; Farías 2014). According to Bowker (2005, 9), this vast list of technologies and practices used by different groups of agents can be classified as "memory regimes" or, "the sets of memory practices that permit both the creation of a continuous, useful past and the transmission sub rosa of information, stories, and practices from our wild, discontinuous, ever-changing past." Understanding memory as a regime is a valuable contribution to the analysis of climatic narratives. First, it conceives memory as a set of material practices to describe the past collectively, beyond individual acts. Second, conceiving of memory as a regime allows the identification of certain homogeneities in which the past is described, enabling the coexistence of multiple schemes of memory simultaneously.

Memory regimes are never tension-free. Similar forms of past constructions, for example those unfolding from scientific schemes, can lead to different creations and explanations of the past—take as an example the previous discussion about the inaugural act of the Anthropocene and how diverse the arguments and narrations are. Similarly, different memory regimes sustained on different types of practices and standards clash when creating coherent causal explanations of past narratives. Think about an alternative world creation—for example, the Andean notion of *Pachakuti*, or "the disruption of the universe," used to understand the cyclical condition of the cosmos and its permanent renewal through catastrophic events (see Rivera Cusicanqui, 1991)—versus a scientific explanation of disasters. Both emphasize the causes that lead to a catastrophe, but in order to do so, they appeal to a completely different set of practices, technologies, narratives, and even temporalities.

Different memory practices and regimes lead to different understandings of the Anthropocene as material reality—a period of increasing global heating more prone to extreme events. Nevertheless, my goal here is not to talk in detail about the inaugural event of the Anthropocene. Instead, I will put the attention on climatic controversies emerging in locations affected by the consequences of massive carbon dioxide emissions. The increasing risks of local climatic-induced disasters like extreme floods are an expression of our current planetary crisis. However, just like for the Anthropocene, the starting point of such events is neither clearly defined nor delimited. When does a catastrophe such as a flash flood take place? Is it when the massive runoff made by mud and water hits the first settlements? Or is it when the local government authorizes the construction of houses near the exposed areas? Or is it even earlier, when industrial development in Western countries led to the release of unmeasurable tons of carbon dioxide into the atmosphere? Or is it the mere existence of humankind that can be blamed for the possibility of disasters?

Furthermore, what sort of conclusions about the Anthropocene can we make by searching for concrete cases of climatic narratives? If we understand the Anthropocene as a unified event with a single, clear inaugural act, does not this necessarily imply agreeing on only one possible explanation for the occurrence of extreme events? On the other hand, if we accept the temporal differences and narratives about the Anthropocene, would not this mean expanding the very concept of time for this new geological epoch, and including even other types of world arrangements that escape the traditional scientific paradigm?

Early-Warning Systems and Earth-Beings

To investigate the previous questions further, I explore two cases of flood controversies in the region of Ancash, Peru, involving Lakes 513 and Palcacocha. Both water bodies are located in the Cordillera Blanca, the largest continuous mountain area of tropical glaciers in the world (Brugger et al. 2010). They provide water for inhabitants of villages and cities downstream that run diverse economic activities mostly associated with agriculture and tourism. The latter is a direct result of the proximity of the

Cordillera Blanca's renowned hiking trails and archaeological centers, which attract thousands of tourists every year.

During the last century, the region of Ancash has faced a significant number of glacier-based disasters, particularly glacial lake outburst floods (GLOF), due to the increasing process of ice melting and the rapid formation of new, fragile mountain lakes. In 1941, a massive runoff of mud and water coming from Palcacocha and originated by ice detachment destroyed a considerable part of Huaraz, Ancash's capital, and took the lives of around 5,000 inhabitants. In 1962, a glacial avalanche coming from Huascarán, Peru's highest mountain, struck the city Ranrahirca and killed 2,000 people. Similarly, the 1970 earthquake of Ancash led to another avalanche from Huascarán, this time burying the city of Yungay and killing more than 15,000 people; it is remembered as the worst glacial disaster in history. In 2010, an outburst flood coming from lagoon 513 struck the village of Hualcán and the city of Carhuaz, destroying roads and farms. In total, around 30,000 people have died over the last century due to glacial disasters in the region (Carey 2010).

These events gained the attention of the scientific community, which has been conducting long-standing work to monitor glaciers in the zone (Carey et al. 2016). These studies have shown a 23% decline in the glaciated area over the last 40 years, forecasting future water scarcity problems (Brugger et al. 2010). Moreover, scientists expect that meltwater flowing directly to mountain lakes increases the chances of floods, which raises the risk of these hazards for cities like Huaraz and Carhuaz.

Scientific findings have raised awareness among local and regional authorities, which have allocated resources for the construction of mitigation infrastructure to reduce flood risks. Huaraz is currently undergoing several technological implementations to cope with another GLOF from Lake Palcacocha that could seriously damage a city that has seen its population increase tenfold since the last event in 1941. Similarly, authorities from Carhuaz have been working since the 2010 flood to reduce the impacts that a new outburst flood from Lake 513 could have on a considerable part of the city. In both cases, the detachment of ice glaciers and landslides over the lakes could lead to the collapse of the earthen dam holding back the water and produce a massive runoff that could take thousands of lives and cost millions in material losses.

Efforts made in this regard, however, have not been tension-free. In 2017, the international non-governmental organization (NGO) CARE Peru, together with local glaciologists, academics from Zurich University, and the Swiss Agency for Development and Cooperation, installed an early-warning system near Lake 513 to automatically notify the authorities about overflows coming from the lake and thus reduce the consequences of a flood like the one in 2010. Despite the efforts made by the organizations to create awareness among the population about the relevance of the early-warning systems for cities like Carhuaz, the presence of this technology led to several conflicts with local groups. Local farmers saw the installation of the early-warning system as a direct threat to their environment and the ultimate explanation for climatic anomalies and disasters. For them, the main danger they were facing had little to do with glacial ice melting, but was linked with scarce precipitations that have been affecting the region over the last decades—a direct consequence of climate change trends threatening local agriculture and livestock. Foreign technology near the water sources was, according to the farmers, the ultimate explanation of a particularly severe drought experienced that year, as the equipment "blocked" the rain by sending signals to the sky. Local testimonies commonly say that, with this argument in mind, an angry mass of *comuneros* (members of the peasant communities) went to the lake some months after the installation of the system and destroyed the boosting antennas connecting the station to Carhuaz.

The destruction of the system caused great consternation among the urban population, who demanded that the local authorities

[Fig. 1] Remains of one of the destroyed antennas in Shonqi Pampa, an area used by local peasants for cattle grazing. At the back: Hualcán Mountain, where Lake 513 is located (Source: Usón 2020)

bring legal proceedings against the people responsible. Finding the perpetrators, however, has not been an easy task. While citizens from Carhuaz blame the population of Hualcán, the nearby rural locality upstream, for considering them the originators of the rumors against the early-warning system, the inhabitants of Hualcán say that the destruction was due to an orchestrated effort among communities from other places in the region, including nearby areas like Yungay and Vicos. When asked by authorities, people simply answer: "it was the *comuneros.*" This anecdote exemplifies the remarkable lack of information surrounding this case, making the prosecution of those responsible highly improbable, if not impossible.

Despite its ominous outcome, this incident is by no means surprising or singular. Peasant communities in Ancash and Peru in general have dealt historically with the environmental impacts of national and international extractive projects in their lands, which, using "foreign" technology, overexploit hydrological sources and threaten water availability and quality (see Salas

 Carreño 2008; Bebbington 2009; Li 2015). Furthermore, for peasant communities living in the region, elements like glaciers and lakes are not only things but Earth-beings—in the words of Marisol de la Cadena (2012, 342) "sentient entities whose material existence—and that of the world to which they belong—is currently threatened by the neoliberal wedding of capital and the state." The combination of reluctance over foreign projects and an "animist"[3] vision of nature sets the proper scenario for rejecting any sort of technological device. Scientists and public organizations have struggled with similar situations in several places in the region. Recently, *comuneros* from the locality of Musho expelled an expedition of scientists from Ohio State University led by the prestigious glaciologist Lonnie Thompson, who was collecting some ice samples from Huascarán. Some versions say that the *comuneros* accused them of working for a mining company looking for gold. Others argue that they were installing similar technology to that in Lake 513, which would also send secret signs to the sky to stop the rains. Glaciologists and engineers tell stories like this repeatedly from other regions where traces of once-existing meteorological and scientific infrastructure have been impossible to find.

3 Traditionally, anthropology has understood animism as the epistemology that believes that all things and entities—including humans, animals and objects—have an animated substance that can ultimately allow the interconnection between them. In recent decades, anthropologists have agreed upon the limited vision that the classical notion of animism presents due to its uncritically assumed Western and modernist notions of human and the environment, and the inflexible dichotomies of nature/culture, human/non-human, and body/soul they entail. Scholars have proposed instead alternative—or complementary—concepts such as relational epistemology (Bird-David 1999), perspectivism (Viveiros de Castro 1998), or modes of identification (Descola 2006). All these notions share the idea of overcoming the projection of human sociality onto the non-human world and expanding the epistemic-ontological conditions shaping the relations that humans and other-than-humans might have. For a deeper critical review of the notion of animism in the Andean world, see Stensrud (2019).

International Emissions

Despite the enormous skepticism of certain groups over foreign organizations and technology in Ancash, the region has also been the scenario of unique alliances between local and international actors fighting against CO_2 emissions. After the 1941 flood that struck Huaraz, the Lake Palcacocha case once again gained international attention when a landslide from one of its lateral moraines impacted the lake in 2003 and caused a moderate outburst flood downstream. Although the event did not result in significant losses for the population, it raised the awareness of the US National Aeronautics and Space Administration (NASA), whose public statements warning about an imminent GLOF in Huaraz led to a disproportionate media response that caused panic among inhabitants. Local authorities were highly critical of the reaction of the US agency, claiming their response to the event sparked unnecessary fear (Carey 2010). Either way, the controversy around the flood reactivated a forgotten discussion of public opinion: whether the mitigation measures taken so far were appropriate for coping with the destructive consequences that a GLOF coming from the lake might pose to the city (Huggel et al. 2020). It also gave space within Ancash's society to another highly relevant discussion: the accelerated rate that glaciers were melting in the region and the impact that climate change might have on this matter.

In November of 2015 a farmer and mountain guide named Saúl Lliuya from Llupa, a small farming village near Huaraz, filed a lawsuit against the German company Rhenish-Westphalian Power Plant (RWE), the second-biggest electricity producer in Europe and one of the leading carbon emitters in the history of the continent. Supported by the German environmental NGO German Watch, Saúl Lliuya sustained his accusation using Richard Heede's (2014) research on what he calls "the carbon majors," the 90 global companies that produced almost two-thirds of the carbon emissions since the Industrial Revolution. According to Heede's

[Fig. 2] Panoramic view of Lake Palcacocha from one of its dams. On the left side: part of the early-warning system installed in 2019. At the center: rubber pipes used to drain the water from the lake (Source: Usón 2020)

findings, RWE has contributed around 0.5 percent of global anthropic emissions. These arguments were used by Saúl Lliuya and German Watch to blame the company for being directly responsible for climate fluctuations experienced over the last centuries and, thereby, for considerably increasing the chances of an outburst flood coming from Palcacocha. They demanded that RWE reimburse 0.5% of the costs for building a new flood barrier upstream—mitigation work with an estimated cost of US$2.5 million.

The Peruvian farmer and the NGO took the case to a local German court, where it was initially dismissed. However, it was later presented at the Higher Regional Court of Hamm in 2015, making the demand admissible and allowing it to continue in November 2017 (Huggel et al. 2020). The process is currently at the evidentiary stage, which means that further information needs to be collected to certify the plausibility of the accusation. According to some conversations I had with Saúl Lliuya, during 2020 the judge leading the case will visit Palcacocha together with a team of scientists and specialists to collect more data for the trial. They will also conduct an audience in Huaraz together with RWE and the complaining party. With this visit to Ancash, the regional court expects to decide whether floods produced by the melting glacier threatens Saúl Lliuya's environment, and to what extent RWE's emissions contributed to the glacial melt that increased flooding risks in Huaraz.

This case is a fundamental breakthrough for discussions regarding climate justice. It is the first time in history that a national court admitted a lawsuit against a company accused of being responsible for climate damages in a part of the globe outside its jurisdiction. Thus, it sets a precedent for a third party not operating in the affected country to be blamed for the global consequences of its emissions. If the German court recognizes the connection between the emissions of RWE and the increasing flash-flood risks in Huaraz, it will allow the development of further cases connecting one particular carbon emitter to concrete, local climatic disasters. This case can ultimately set an example for further legal discussions on responsibility and liability for climate litigation—an increasingly growing field that still presents several operational gaps for both national and international resolutions (Marjanac and Patton 2018; Huggel et al. 2020).

Floods as Boundary Objects

The two examples above offer remarkable insights for the discussion about memory practices and regimes in times of the Anthropocene and their consequences for preparing for unknown futures. They show how different processes of narrating the past can lead to diverse understandings of current events together with various forms of coping with them. The heterogeneity of memory practices presents several challenges for dealing with future disasters jointly: How can narrations of the past that incorporate different meanings and even agents become coherent? How can different world projects communicate with each other?

Susan Leigh Star and James Griesemer (1989) addressed similar questions when researching the scientific practices behind the work of museums. The authors analyzed the operations of the Museum of Vertebrate Zoology in Berkeley, California, a renowned institution of natural history working as a repository of regional specimens of vertebrates, where the work of scientists and amateur collectors comes together. According to Leigh Star and Griesemer, two main factors contribute to the proper functioning of the museum and the creation of alliances among heterogeneous groups of agents. The authors emphasize the definition of methods standardization, namely, a collection of standards, protocols, and even devices that ensure the participation of the diverse range of agents involved, including scientists, collectors, local animal trappers, and financial supporters. From their conducted research, Leigh Star and Griesemer conclude that the development of what they call boundary objects is a fundamental aspect of developing joint work. Boundary objects are plastic enough to adapt to local needs and understandings, but robust enough to maintain a shared identity despite their plasticity across different places. Common boundary objects are those used in different worlds simultaneously to produce shareable understanding—in the case of the museum to collaborate for representing nature—even if they do not agree on what the object itself is (Leigh Star and Griesemer 1989, 393). They can include specimens, field notes, museums themselves, and maps, which can be locally appropriated and abstractly conceived (Leigh Star and Griesemer 1989, 410).

For the purposes of mountain guide Saúl Lliuya's case, it is possible to find some traces of methods standardization and boundary objects. Because the courts operate under Western epistemologies derived from Enlightenment traditions, Saúl Lliuya is required to scientifically prove that the consequences of

RWE's emissions are directly affecting the security of Huaraz. He does find support in a large group of scientists and experts who are willing to demonstrate the connection between anthropogenic emissions and glacial ice melting. The narrative work—i.e., the sense-giving about the historical impact of RWE on the transformation of lifestyles in Huaraz—has to be achieved through scientific evidence, including hydroclimatic data and analysis embodied in memory devices such as temperature charts, precipitation records, and glacial modeling giving signs of climatic fluctuations over the last centuries. However, this narration work also requires the registering of life stories evidencing the impact that climatic transformation has had for local lives in the short and medium term.

In this sense, the definition of boundary objects has to be general enough to allow common discussions, but sufficiently plastic to be signified differently according to the context. Our example of outburst floods can be understood as a remarkable example of this. The destructive capacity of such events is large enough to be relevant in different contexts, whether for the inhabitants of Huaraz and Llupa or the members of the regional court in Hamm. However, the form in which the event relates to the past narratives of agents is diverse. Saúl Lliuya focuses on previous floods to argue the consequences that a possible outburst of Palcacocha may produce in the region, together with the responsibility that companies like RWE should assume for coping with them. For the environmental NGO German Watch, however, a potential flood is a form of exemplifying through a local case the consequences that the historical emissions of companies like RWE have had on a global scale. RWE, on the other hand, sees the increase in flood risks as the result of the lifestyles assumed by a considerable part of the population (at least from the so-called "Global North"). Under this view, a search for those responsible for the emissions and, thereby, the current climate trends, is not only impossible but unfair—an argument that ultimately reminds us of the famous phrase of Ulrich Beck (1997, 14): "Society becomes a laboratory with nobody responsible for the outcomes of experiments." It is through the consideration of all of these perspectives that the German Regional Court must evaluate whether the connection between greenhouse gases and flood risk is solid enough to find RWE guilty under German law. The court must determine if other cases in the history of the German justice system could sustain Saúl Lliuya's lawsuit, translating the elements involved in Palcacocha's flood risks to the German jurisdiction.

The remarkable aspect of Saúl Lliuya's case is its capacity to connect a local glacial retreatment with a global scale of discussion. It has the possibility of tracing centuries of carbon emission into the atmosphere within local stories of glacial lakes' outburst floods and risk preparedness. This connection requires a standardized form of narration for the boundary object—the outburst flooding—that is re-signified not just as an accelerated process of glacial melting due to the actions of humankind, but also as the direct result of a specific set of actors, the "carbon majors," to use Heede's (2014) term. By standardizing the causes of the flood, the connection made by Saúl Lliuya makes possible the process of temporal acceleration and compression of the Anthropocene, connecting centuries of carbon emission into the atmosphere with millions of years of geostory, now embodied in a company with names, offices, and electric stations. Accepting RWE's responsibility in this case means, therefore, recognizing the company as a geological force.

Disasters as Ontological Disputes

The case of Saúl Lliuya builds upon a common understanding of a possible GLOF and the capacity of presenting such risk in different settings. But what happens when the necessary conditions for discussing and generating a shared narrative are not there? What happens when differences among world projects are so vast that there is not even a possibility for dialogue? The aforementioned destruction of the early-warning system in Lake 513, led by local *comuneros,* shows precisely this.

Anthropological studies have explored how disagreements among actors problematize common arrangements of the world (Tironi 2014; Venturini 2010). Disagreements, which vary in magnitude and intensity, include not only institutional discrepancies (how the world is ruled and controlled) and epistemic differences (how the world is represented), but even what some authors have defined as ontological disputes (how the world is created). Authors like Mario Blaser (2013; 2014) have addressed the idea of ontological conflicts to explore the differences produced when Indigenous explanations and configurations of the world are forced to fit into universalist efforts of modernity. Based on Isabelle Stengers' (2011) concept of divergence—i.e., practices by which entities remain distinct in their heterogeneity as they come together—Blaser and Marisol de la Cadena (2017) argue that some world projects are so dissimilar that they do not leave space for discussions, arousing the emergency of "uncommons." Unlike commons, which can be understood as non-human agents tightly bounded with a community creating collective forms of domain, the uncommons refers to the incapacity of aligning projects from different domains, leading to irreconcilable worlds obliterating any project of shared ground. This uncommunality can ultimately jeopardize efforts for successful communication between various agents.

Ontological differences, however, do not entirely restrict efforts to understand when concepts originally used by the other might not have proper substitutes to translate from one relational world to another. In his study on different ontological arrangements explaining the climatic conditions of the Amazonas, Aníbal Arregui (2018) shows how two different worlds, embodied by the figures of the climatologist Antonio Nobre and the Yanomami shaman Davi Kopenawa, try to connect with each other to explain their knowledge and experiences to a broad, varied public. Both share a common assumption, namely, that the destruction of forest trees affects the rain patterns in the Amazonas. But they reach that conclusion from two completely different world arrangements. Instead of neglecting each other's perspective, they accept working together despite the lack of common terms. Nobre, on the one hand, is willing to cope with the spirits of the forest to be found in Kopenawa's world, despite his incapacity to grasp them as scientific elements. Kopenawa, on the other hand, is open to work with white people's disembodied forms of knowledge such as books and satellite images, even though they do not make sense when explaining his own relationship with the forest. Arregui proposes Viveiros de Castro's (2004) concept of controlled equivocation to explain how this exchange might take place. The term refers to a gap in knowledge that is consciously accepted to solve the complete lack of conceptual correspondence. The communicating parties share a common assumption, but they cannot fully grasp the meaning of their explanations. Instead of looking for synonyms—"a co-referential representation"—to understand what the other means, they "avoid losing sight of the difference concealed within equivocal homonyms" (Viveiros de Castro 2004, 7). By doing so, they leave open the possibility of misunderstanding without closing the doors for communication.

The idea of ontological disputes gives some insights into the destruction of the meteorological station as an inflection point of disagreement. In the Lake 513 case, divergences regarding disasters are twofold. First, there is the very understanding of a disaster: while for the inhabitants of Carhuaz the ultimate threat is the massive runoff as a consequence of global warming and glaciers retreating, for local farmers living off agriculture in the upper parts of the mountain, disaster is mostly related to water shortage. The second divergence is related to the causes of the disaster. For the scientific community, as for Saúl Lliuya, the accelerated process of ice melting is intrinsically related to the exponential emissions from hydrocarbons entering the atmosphere. Whereas for the peasant communities, the lack of precipitations affecting the zone is seen as resulting mostly from the installation of foreign technology, which threatens the existence of earth-beings such as mountains and lakes.

Solutions for these disagreements still have not been found. The local government in Carhuaz fears that a new early-warning system may suffer the same fate as its predecessor. Some local peasants still think that foreign technology might be the entrance door for mining companies and environmental degradation. Under this scenario, speculative work with controlled equivocation gives us some hope for conceiving a common ground for dialogue. Although scientists and local peasants conceive different things when thinking about disasters, they do share a common way of seeing it: the disruptive condition that disasters entail. By sharing such disruptiveness—i.e. the consequences of scarce precipitations and imminent GLOFs from Lake 513—both groups could find a common area of understanding, even if they must accept their incapacity to fully grasp the other's explanations. It is a form of finding a meeting point in the midst of differences—not to impede the relation but to find it and impel it (Viveiros de Castro 2004). If both narrations of the past can partially connect, whether by building bridges between them or by creating a new regime that incorporates their diversity, is still unknown. Equally unknown are the necessary mechanisms to avoid the imposition of one memory regime over another. Nevertheless, controlled equivocation might bring some hope for enhancing dialogue and mutual recognition among actors in cases where essential dissimilarities are the norm.

Towards a Cosmopolitical Lecture of the Anthropocene

The cases of Lake 513 and Lake Palcacocha are valuable demonstrations of how different forms of narrating the past, developed by several world projects, can clash with each other, sometimes in apparently irreconcilable ways. Both cases show us, following

Latour (2017), that it does not make sense to talk about the *anthropos* in the Anthropocene as a joint project of humankind, as a unified agency. The Anthropocene demands instead that we break down humanity into a vast list of world projects, interests, and, as a matter of concern for this article, forms of narrating past events. By engaging with this diversity of narratives, we are accepting the relevance of all past constructions for making sense of our heterogeneous presents. Universality, as Latour argues, has to be composed rather than assumed. The production of this common world, termed by Latour (2004) and Stengers (2010) as cosmopolitics, is a permanent dispute among divergent world projects that collide into each other in a constant struggle for visibility and recognition. In this manner, overcoming the idea of a unified memory implies overcoming the notion of a unified humanity.

Cases like Palcacocha and Lake 513 should be studied to explore our ability for processing all their stories, connections, and transformations of agents into their environments. They show us how memory and knowledge regimes in the Anthropocene work to make sense of those transformations and relations, without simplifying the stories of its components into larger narratives but also without reducing everything to mere stories without any sort of connection. And most importantly, the previously exposed cases help us to reflect on the possibility of locating meeting points that allow us to connect the different memory regimes that we can find along the way. Further research on cases like Palcacocha and Lake 513 can enable us to propose connections that, albeit only partially, could help us to integrate diverse world arrangements into a common geostory when thinking about the consequences—and origins—of climatic disasters.

I would like to express gratitude to the members of the Museum Lab and the City Lab of the Institute for European Ethnology as well as the IRI THESys' PhD colloquium group of the Humboldt University of Berlin and participants of the Atlas of the Anthropocene Symposium. Their feedback and comments were fundamental for the elaboration and improvement of the arguments expressed in this article (I retain full responsibility for the content). I am also deeply grateful to Ignacio Farías, Réka Gál and Petra Löffler for their insightful and valuable comments on earlier versions of this article. Special thanks to all the people from Huaraz, Carhuaz, Llupa, Hualcán, and places nearby in Ancash that agreed to be interviewed for this research. This work was possible thanks to the generous support of the Friedrich Ebert Foundation's Doctoral Funding Program.

References

Agostinho, Daniela. 2015. "Flooded with Memories: Risk Cultures, the Big Flood of 1953 and the Visual Resonance of World War Two." In *Hazardous Future: Disaster, Representation and the Assessment of Risk*, edited by Gil Isabel Capeloa and Christoph Wulf, 265–86. Berlin: De Gruyter. doi: 10.1515/9783110406610.

Arregui, Aníbal G. 2018. "Embodying Equivocations: Ecopolitical Mimicries of Climate Science and Shamanism." *Anthropological Theory*, February. doi: 10.1177/1463499617753335.

Bebbington, Anthony. 2009. "The New Extraction: Rewriting the Political Ecology of the Andes?" *NACLA Report on the Americas* 42 (5): 12–20. doi: 10.1080/10714839.2009.11722221.

Beck, Ulrich. 1997. "The Politics of Risk Society." In *The Politics of Risk Society*, edited by Jane Franklin, 1st edition, 8–22. Cambridge: Polity.

Bergson, Henri. 1911. *Matter and Memory*. London: Swan Sonnenschein.

Bird-David, Nurit. 1999. "'Animism' Revisited: Personhood, Environment, and Relational Epistemology" *Current Anthropology* 40: 67–91. doi: 10.1086/200061.

Blaser, Mario. 2013. "Ontological Conflicts and the Stories of Peoples in Spite of Europe: Toward a Conversation on Political Ontology." *Current Anthropology* 54 (5): 547–68. doi: 10.1086/672270.

Blaser, Mario. 2014. "Ontology and Indigeneity: On the Political Ontology of Heterogeneous Assemblages." *Cultural Geographies* 21 (1): 49–58. doi: 10.1177/1474474012462534.

Blaser, Mario, and Marisol de la Cadena. 2017. "The Uncommons: An Introduction." *Anthropologica* 59 (2): 185–93. doi: 10.3138/anth.59.2.t01.

Bowker, Geoffrey C. 2005. *Memory Practices in the Sciences*. Cambridge: MIT Press.

Brugger, Julie, Kate Dunbar, Christine Jurt, and Ben Orlove. 2010. "Global Warming and Changing Water Resources: Perceptions of Glacier Retreat in Mountain Regions." *Anthropology News* 51 (2): 23–24. doi: 10.1111/j.1556-3502.2010.51223.x.

Callon, Michel, and Bruno Latour. 1981. "Unscrewing the Big Leviathan: How Actors Macro-Structure Reality and how Sociologists Help them to do so." In *Advances in Social Theory and Methodology*, edited by Karen Knorr-Cetina and Aaron V. Cicourel, 276–303. Boston, MA: Routledge & Kegan Paul.

Carey, Mark. 2010. *In the Shadow of Melting Glaciers: Climate Change and Andean Society*. Oxford: Oxford University Press.

Carey, Mark, Rodney Garrard, Courtney Cecale, Wouter Buytaert, Christian Huggel, and Mathias Vuile. 2016. "Climbing for Science and Ice: From Hans Kinzl and Mountaineering Glaciology to Citizen Science in the Cordillera Blanca." *Revista de Glaciares y Ecosistemas de Montaña* 1 (1): 59–72. www.atmos.albany.edu/facstaff/mathias/pubs/Carey_et_al_2017.pdf.

Crutzen, Paul J., and Eugene F. Stoermer. 2000. "The "Anthropocene"." *Global Change Newsletter* 41: 17–18. www.igbp.net/publications/globalchangemagazine/globalchangemagazine/globalchangenewslettersno4159.5.5831d9ad13275d51c098000309.html.

de la Cadena, Marisol 2012. "Indigenous Cosmopolitics in the Andes: Conceptual Reflections Beyond 'Politics.'" *Cultural Anthropology* 25 (2): 334–70. doi: 10.1111/j.1548-1360.2010.01061.x.

Descola, Philippe. 2006. *Beyond Nature and Culture*. Chicago: The University of Chicago Press.

Dlugokencky, Ed J., Brad D. Hall, Stephen A. Montzka, Geoff Dutton, Jens Mühle, and James W. Elkins. 2019. "Atmospheric Composition." *State of the Climate in 2018, Chapter 2: Global Climate. Bulletin of the American Meteorological Society*, 100 (9): 48–50.

Farías, Ignacio 2014. "Planes Maestros como Cosmogramas." *Revista Pléyade* 14: 119–42. www.revistapleyade.cl/wp-content/uploads/6.-Far%C3%ADas-12-1.pdf.

Heede, Richard. 2014. "Tracing Anthropogenic Carbon Dioxide and Methane Emissions to Fossil Fuel and Cement Producers, 1854–2010." *Climatic Change* 122: 229–41. doi: 10.1007/s10584-013-0986-y.

Huggel, Christian, Mark Carey, Adam Emmer, Holger Frey, Noah Walker-Crawford, and Ivo Wallimann-Helmer. 2020. "Anthropogenic Climate Change and Glacier Lake Outburst Flood Risk: Local and Global Drivers and Responsibilities for the Case of Lake Palcacocha, Peru." *Natural Hazards and Earth System Sciences Discussions*, 20: 2175–93. doi: 10.5194/nhess-2020-44.

Juneja, Monica, and Gerrit Jasper Schenk. 2014. "Viewing Disasters. Myth, History, Iconography and Media Across Europe and Asia." In *Disaster as Image: Iconographies and Media Strategies Across Europe and Asia*, edited by Monica Juneja and Gerrit Jasper Schenk, 7–42. Regensburg: Schnell & Steiner.

Latour, Bruno. 2004. "Whose Cosmos, which Cosmopolitics? Comments on the Peace Terms of Ulrich Beck." *Common Knowledge* 10: 450–62. www.bruno-latour.fr/sites/default/files/92-BECK_GB.pdf.

Latour, Bruno. 2017. *Facing Gaia: Eight Lectures on the New Climatic Regime*. 1st edition. Cambridge: Polity.

Leigh Star, Susan, and James R. Griesemer. 1989. "Institutional Ecology, 'Translations' and Boundary Objects: Amateurs and Professionals in Berkeley's Museum of Vertebrate Zoology, 1907-39." *Social Studies of Science* 19 (3): 387–420. doi: 10.1177/030631289019003001.

Li, Fabiana. 2015. *Unearthing Conflict: Corporate Mining, Activism, and Expertise in Peru*. Durham, NC: Duke University Press.

Lovelock, James, and Lynn Margulis. (1973) 2016. "Atmospheric Homeostasis by and for the Biosphere: The Gaia Hypothesis". *Tellus* 26 (1–2): 2–10. doi: 10.3402/tellusa.v26i1-2.9731.

Marjanac, Sophie and Lindene Patton. 2018. "Extreme Weather Event Attribution Science and Climate Change Litigation: An Essential Step in the Causal Chain?". *Journal of Energy & Natural Resources Law*: 1–34. doi: 10.1080/02646811.2018.1451020.

Middleton, David, and Steve D. Brown. 2005. *The Social Psychology of Experience: Studies in Remembering and Forgetting*. London: SAGE.

Morton, Timothy. 2013. *Hyperobjects. Philosophy and Ecology After the End of the World*. Minneapolis: University of Minnesota Press.

November, Valérie, Eduardo Camacho-Hübner, and Bruno Latour. 2010. "Entering a Risky Territory: Space in the Age of Digital Navigation." *Environment and Planning D: Society and Space* 28 (4): 581–99. doi: 10.1068/d10409.

Povinelli, Elizabeth A. 2016. *Geontologies: A Requiem to Late Liberalism*. Durham, NC: Duke University Press Books.

Rivera Cusicanqui, Silvia. 1991. *Pachakuti: Los Aymaras de Bolivia frente a Medio Milenio de Colonialismo*. La Paz: Chukiyawu.

Salas Carreño, Guillermo. 2008. *Dinámica Social y Minería. Familias Pastoras de Puna y la Presencia del Proyecto Antamina (1997-2002)*. Lima: Instituto de Estudios Peruanos.

Stengers, Isabelle. 2010. *Cosmopolitics I*. Minneapolis: University of Minnesota Press.

Stengers, Isabelle. 2011. "Comparison as a Matter of Concern." *Common Knowledge* 17 (1): 48–63. doi: 10.1215/0961754X-2010-035.

Stensrud, Astrid. 2019. "Los Peregrinos Urbanos en Qoyllurit'i y el Juego Mimético de Miniaturas." *Anthropologica* 28 (28): 39–65. dialnet.unirioja.es/servlet/articulo?codigo=5042107

Tironi, Manuel. 2014. "Atmospheres of Indagation: Disasters and the Politics of Excessiveness." *The Sociological Review* 62 (S1): 114–34. doi: 10.1111/1467-954X.12126.

Venturini, Tommaso. 2010. "Diving in Magma: How to Explore Controversies with Actor-Network Theory." *Public Understanding of Science* 19 (3): 258–73. doi: 10.1177/0963662509102694.

Viveiros de Castro, Eduardo. 1998. *Cosmological Perspectivism in Amazonia and Elsewhere: Four Lectures Given in the Department of Social Anthropology, Cambridge University, February–March 1998*. Manchester: HAU Books.

Viveiros de Castro, Eduardo. 2004. "Perspectival Anthropology and the Method of Controlled Equivocation." *Tipití: Journal of the Society for the Anthropology of Lowland South America* 2 (1): 3–22. https://digitalcommons.trinity.edu/tipiti/vol2/iss1/1/.

Zalasiewicz, Jan, Colin N. Waters, Anthony D. Barnosky, et al. 2015. "Colonization of the Americas, 'Little Ice Age' Climate, and Bomb-Produced Carbon: Their Role in Defining the Anthropocene." *Anthropocene Review* 2 (2): 117–27. doi: 10.1177/2053019615587056.

Archipalego

Anna Zilahi

The sliding of two tectonic plates into one-another is subsequently no longer subversive. No matter whether we're satisfied with the explanation, the dilemma of evasion or collision does not rely on contingency. Which will curve upwards into the relief of terrain, and which will submerge beneath the cloak? The isle-arc gathers within a pleat both its past and future: my first breath, as the air forces a path through the mucus, but I am my suffocation too. There are things that even deep sea trenches cannot swallow, it quietly spills its fertile poison along the fault line. To break free, the volatile matter drives the permanent upward. It is not part of the transforming landscape. The permanent is also volatile, but this does not alleviate the entrapment within a phase transition. Heat suddenly floods the plates tautened across one another. The volatile slowly gathers, it impedes light's path as it condenses. The sea of clouds falls back. If the water-level surpasses itself, it sweeps the permanent beneath itself.

Translated by Owen Good

ANTHROPOCENE

GEOLOGY

LONG DURATION

(UN)FOUNDING FICTIONS

MODERN LITERATURE

[3]

Writing the *longue durée*: Foundational Fictions and the Anthropocene

Jörg Dünne

From the discovery of geologic "deep time," nineteenth-century literary imaginations of modernity articulated connections between the long timescale of the Earth's history and the history of the present. Some elements of Argentina's geologic history that have played a decisive role in the development of paleontology have been used by authors as varied as Honoré de Balzac and Florentino Ameghino as the imaginary foundation of present civilizations or nations in deep time. Unlike such appropriations of the deep past, contemporary literature no longer uses geologic time in order to anchor the present in the past, but instead to question the foundational character of geologic dynamics at the threshold of the new epoch called the "Anthropocene."

The following considerations are about the relation of modern literature to the past, especially to the long-gone past or what is known as "deep time."[1] They will lead from nineteenth-century France to several literary sites of "deep history" in Argentina, where I will not only deal with the history of the Earth but also with the intersection of different timescales in the present moment, which has lately been described as the geological epoch of the "Anthropocene."

I. Some Preliminaries About the "Anthropocene" and its Relevance to Narrative Fiction

The by now well-established concept of the "Anthropocene"[2] was introduced to designate a geological epoch in which the human impact on the biosphere can be perceived stratigraphically in a new geologic formation of the Earth's surface. Despite its shallow depth in comparison with the entire crust of the Earth and its infinitesimal duration in relation to the more than 4,000 million years since the Earth was formed, this new stratum can be detected, among other factors, due to the presence of radioactive elements such as plutonium, produced by the use of nuclear

1 The talk this text is based upon was first presented in English at the symposium "Atlas of the Anthropocene" in June 2019 and then translated into Spanish, the language in which it was presented on several occasions in Argentina in October 2019 and eventually published under the title "Escribiendo el 'tiempo profundo': Ficciones fundacionales y el Antropoceno" (Dünne 2020a). This English text is a modified and slightly shortened retranslation of the Spanish version. All English translations of the Spanish literary texts in this article are my own. I would like to thank Michael Thomas Taylor for editing the text.

2 The concept began to spread after a seminal article by Paul J. Crutzen (2002); for the subsequent debate in geology, see Zalasiewicz et al. (2019); the transfer to the humanities was established by, among other publications, an influential article by Dipesh Chakrabarty (2009) and Bruno Latour's essay *Facing Gaia* (2017). For a more detailed account of the history of the Anthropocene, see the introduction to this volume.

weapons since the middle of the twentieth century (on the "golden spike" for determining the beginning of the new period, see Anthropocene Working Group 2019). It is by now quite likely that the Anthropocene will officially succeed the Holocene, which currently constitutes the last layer of the International Chronostratigraphic Chart drafted by the International Commission on Stratigraphy (see fig. 1). As this chart shows, the concept of the Anthropocene is inseparable from a certain way of spatializing "deep time" (on this term, see Gould 1987) by the superposition of different vertical strata on the surface of the Earth. I will return to this imagination of temporality as stratification throughout my following reflections.

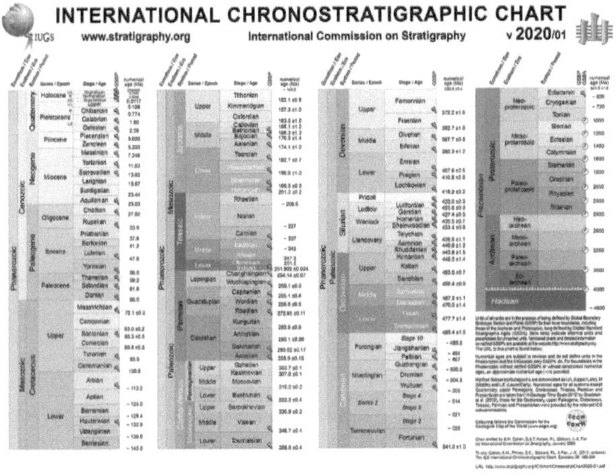

[Fig. 1] International Chronostratigraphic Chart (Source: http://www.stratigraphy.org/ICSchart/ChronostratChart2020-01.jpg)

The transdisciplinary concept of the Anthropocene has provoked a broad and controversial ongoing debate in geology as well as in the humanities (for an overview see Lorimer 2017): one of the issues under debate is whether it is justified to call this new epoch the Anthropocene, with its etymology ("the man-made new") favoring the impact of humanity as a supposedly homogeneous species at the expense of other living species on the planet (see Haraway 2016).[3] One could also ask whether emphasis should rather be placed on the enormous differences between the impact of human societies in the "Global North" and those in the "Global South" since the early modern period,[4] and whether, instead of blaming the whole human species, it would not be more accurate to attribute the responsibility for climate change to the rise of global capitalism—a thesis that led Jason Moore to propose the alternative neologism "Capitalocene" (Moore 2016). Even if the Anthropocene can be questioned in various respects, there are, to my mind, three crucial features of the concept that justify its further use in critical discourse:

- The Anthropocene questions the established distinction between a more or less stable "nature" on the one hand and a changing "culture" on the other, similar to the arguments that have been made about this distinction by anthropologists like Philippe Descola (2013) and sociologists of science like Bruno Latour (2017).
- If used as a tool for critical reflection, it can help distinguish, as has been shown by Dipesh Chakrabarty (2012), between "humans" as a species and "humans" as individual actors, and thus to analyze the rhetoric of the first-person plural implied in the use of "we" during the Anthropocene (see also Stockhammer 2017).
- The Anthropocene allows for a critical reflection on the different temporalities that human beings may experience, from geological deep time to meaningful events at the scale of a human lifespan; in this context, my main concern is the interference of these temporal "scale frames" (see Clark 2015) in cultural and literary narratives.

3 This is the critique made by Donna J. Haraway (2016), who proposes the "Chthulucene" (named after the spider *Pimoa Cthulhu*) as a playful alternative to the Anthropocene.

4 Yusoff (2018) raises the question of to what extent the Anthropocene is a Eurocentric concept in which the traces of the colonial and extractivist history are still present.

In order to develop a literary approach to how significant the deep-time dynamics of the Anthropocene are for the narrative dimension of texts, I will turn to the Indian writer Amitav Ghosh. In a recent essay titled *The Great Derangement: Climate Change and the Unthinkable*, Ghosh asserted categorically: "The longue durée is not the territory of the novel" (Ghosh 2016, 59). Ghosh wonders about the lack of important contemporary novels dealing with climate change, and sees the present not only as a moment of environmental crisis but also a moment of crisis of our literary imagination. For Ghosh, modern novels since (roughly) the nineteenth century, as opposed to premodern epics, "conjure up worlds that become real precisely because of their finitude and distinctiveness. Within the mansion of serious fiction, no one will speak of how the continents were created; nor will they refer to the passage of thousands of years" (Ghosh 2016, 61). Ghosh argues that this makes climate change, as one of the most prominent features of the Anthropocene, almost unthinkable in terms of what he calls "serious" modern literature (by which he means to exclude literary genres like science fiction).

However reductive, Ghosh's thesis has a certain plausibility against the backdrop of the theory of the modern novel. "Agency" in the novel is normally conceived of as agency of human actors who—to take a well-known example in the theory of "plot" according to Russian semiologist of culture Yuri Lotman—are able to transgress a boundary that, normally, they alone are capable of transgressing (Lotman 1977, 217–44). Within this model of agency everything that has to do with the *longue durée*—be it in the sense of Fernand Braudel's environmental history (Braudel 1958) or of the even longer duration of geological deep time—would fall under the category of a "text without plot" in Lotmanian terms, where nothing happens that is relevant for transforming the basic, binary configuration of semantic spaces in the novel. In that sense, Ghosh might be right to say that in the modern novel climate change is, if not unthinkable, at least not relevant at the scale of human agency as a core element for narrative plot structure.

Perhaps the problem is not the absence of deep time in the novel, however, but the conceptual framework for determining what counts as a "plot" at other scales than exclusively the scale of human agency—and, from this point of view, I would like to contest Ghosh's claim. To do so, I will not provide a general overview of how the scientific imagination has discovered deep time (on this topic, see Rudwick 2005 and 2008). Rather, I would like to propose a literary trip through time and space in three exemplary stages, leading from nineteenth-century France to Argentina at the same time and from there to another Argentine setting in the nearby future. The stages of this trip are not connected by any type of influence or direct intertextuality between the texts I will be analyzing but only by material objects and geographic proximity. These connections in turn allow us to describe the superposition of geological and human timescales in cultural and literary imagination throughout the last 200 years, and thus to sketch the prehistory of what could be called the present day's Anthropocenic literature.

II. Paris, circa 1830

Honoré de Balzac's novel *La Peau de chagrin* (*The Magic Skin*, first published in 1831) is arguably less famous for its fantastic plot, about the life span of a young man keen for social success and the story of his pact with the Devil, than for his descriptive opening scene in a "boutique d'antiquaire," the shop of an antiquary. In this shop, Raphaël de Valentin—the protagonist who is about to commit suicide—finds the fragments of various civilizations condensed in a collection of material objects from the past.

At this point, the narrator invokes the French naturalist Georges Cuvier, the founding figure of paleontology and comparative anatomy, delivering what has come to be known as his "éloge de

Cuvier" (eulogy of Cuvier), presenting the scientist as the greatest poet of the nineteenth century:

> Vous êtes-vous jamais lancé dans l'immensité de l'espace et du temps, en lisant les œuvres géologiques de Cuvier? Emporté par son génie, avez-vous plané sur l'abîme sans bornes du passé, comme soutenu par la main d'un enchanteur? En découvrant de tranche en tranche, de couche en couche, sous les carrières de Montmartre ou dans les schistes de l'Oural, ces animaux dont les dépouilles fossilisées appartiennent à des civilisations antédiluviennes, l'âme est effrayée d'entrevoir des milliards d'années, des millions de peuples que la faible mémoire humaine, que l'indestructible tradition divine ont oubliés et dont la cendre entassée à la surface de notre globe y forme les deux pieds de terre qui nous donnent du pain et des fleurs. Cuvier n'est-il pas le plus grand poète de notre siècle? (Balzac 1974, 47)

> Did you ever launch yourself into the vague immensity of space and time as you read the geological works of Cuvier? Carried away by his genius, have you hovered above the fathomless abyss of the past as though sustained by the hand of a magician? Discovering, line upon line, layer upon layer, in the quarries of Montmartre or the gneiss of the Urals, those animals whose fossilized remains belong to antediluvian civilizations, the soul terrified as it perceives the thousand millions of years and of peoples which feeble human memory, even divine indestructible tradition, has forgotten, yet whose dust survives, here on the surface of our earth, in the two feet of soil which give us bread and flowers. Is not Cuvier the greatest poet of our century? (Balzac 1888, 25)

Cuvier is so poetic for Balzac's narrator because he is able to reawaken past civilizations into new life with only a very few fragments from animals' skeletons—a single bone is enough for Cuvier, so the reader is told, to reconstruct a whole prehistoric animal. This capacity of reconstruction from a seemingly inaccessible past is even more relevant against the backdrop of the "catastrophist" understanding of history that Balzac largely adopts from Georges de Cuvier. Based upon his own paleontological investigations, Cuvier developed a theory according to which the history of the Earth had been punctuated by a series of devastating cataclysms, the last of which was the biblical deluge (see Cuvier [1825] 1969). Balzac transfers this geologic catastrophism to another scale by exploiting the polysemy of the French expression "révolution" that, until the nineteenth century, could refer either to "revolutions of the Earth's surface" or to political upheavals, and especially to the 1789 French Revolution that Balzac perceived as a violent disruption of social stability under the ancien régime.

Viewed as a whole, the eulogy *La peau de chagrin* quickly abandons its allusion to deep time and Cuvier's famous theory of catastrophes in favor of the description of other revolutions of a social or political order. Nevertheless, what is especially interesting in this context about Balzac's eulogy is that, if only for a short moment, two very different timescales, namely human history since the French Revolution and the history of the Earth, appear to interact or even to merge. At first view, Balzac's text uses the theory of geological catastrophes only as a drastic metaphor to describe change in cultural history, but a closer look might tell us (as I have argued elsewhere, see Dünne 2016) that the novel of Balzac and of other nineteenth-century French authors such as Jules Verne, Gustave Flaubert, and Émile Zola are deeply affected by the ways in which dealing with geological deep time influences the means available for narratively presenting past events.

The discovery of deep time, as a concept that emerges in the eighteenth century, turns geological time into a privileged model for conceiving other, shorter timescales, as well, which

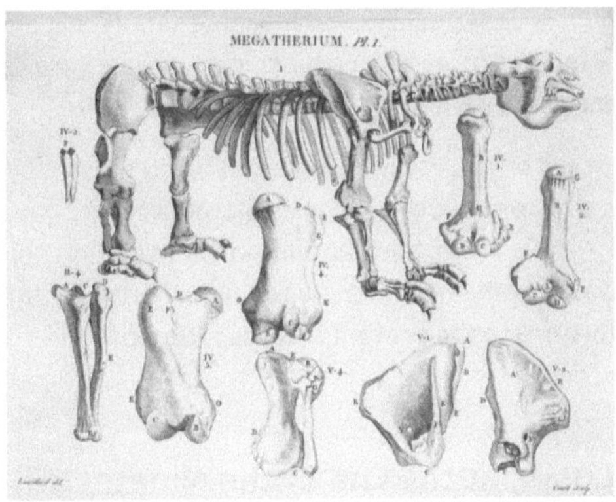

[Fig. 2] *Megatherium* according to Georges Cuvier (Source: Cuvier 1804, s.p.)

contributes to a transformation of the notion of historicity as such.[5] Starting with Balzac, it can be shown not only that the modern literary imagination is inspired by geology but that this imagination goes beyond literary fiction in a narrow sense and extends to political imaginations, inasmuch as the reference to geology makes possible foundational fictions of the social and the political in both Europe and Latin America. To make this argument, I will focus on the material history of the first animal reconstructed by Cuvier and the contribution of this reconstruction to the development of the method of comparative anatomy upon which Balzac's enthusiastic commentary in his eulogy was based (my arguments in the following section rely on Podgorny 2009). This animal—dubbed *Megatherium*—was described by Cuvier for the first time in 1796 in France (see fig. 2) on the basis of drawings of the fossil remains of an animal that had been transported to Madrid in 1789, the year of the French Revolution. These remains had been excavated two years earlier in Argentina, near the Luján river, by a Dominican friar. The

5 For an understanding of history in general as "stratified time," see the historian Reinhart Koselleck (2000). On the geologic as an alternative paradigm for conceiving of a nonlinear temporality in cultural theory, see the groundbreaking study by Manuel De Landa (1997).

Megatherium (a Greek expression meaning simply "big animal") was identified by Cuvier as an extinct species bearing a certain resemblance to today's sloth, but much bigger in size.

The next stage of this voyage will be Luján and the Argentine pampa as sites where deep time has played a constitutive role for literary and political imagination—an imagination pointing not only back in time to earlier stages in the history of the Earth but also forward to the present and the future of a life in the Anthropocene.

III. Luján, at the End of the Nineteenth Century

It is commonplace to say that the history of the Argentine nation and Argentine literature are both bound to a certain type of territoriality, the emblem of which is the flat land of the pampa: this is emptied of its actual inhabitants by settlers and writers alike and is commonly imagined as a desert that needs to be cultivated and civilized in order to become fertile (see Rodríguez 2010). "Civilization," in opposition to "barbarism," is precisely the famous formula invented by the Argentine writer and politician Domingo Faustino Sarmiento in his seminal essay *Facundo* to describe the vast flatlands of the Argentine pampa in 1845 (Sarmiento 2004).

Against this exclusively "horizontal" history of the Argentine territory as a surface of projection for the becoming of a civilized nation, Argentina soon also became a privileged place for the "vertical" discovery of deep time. And it is here that I now come back to the *Megatherium* that Cuvier described in Paris and its fossil bones, which today can be viewed in Madrid in Spain but were originally found near a place called Luján, not far from Buenos Aires (see De Iuliis et al. 2005). In colonial times and also later on, fossil bones of extinct American animals like the *Megatherium* and the *Glypotodon* were first exported to Europe but soon also came to be used in the service of the history of

Argentina: to compensate for the country being such a "young" nation in terms of political history, claims were made to found an Argentine protohistory in deep time long before nation states and other forms of political organization.

The keenest attempt at such a "vertical" foundational fiction for the Argentine nation in deep time is without any doubt the hypothesis of the Argentine naturalist and paleontologist Florentino Ameghino (on Ameghino's research into paleontology, see Podgorny 2015), himself born in Luján, where the first *Megatherium* skeleton was found. Inspired by the discovery of these fossils, at the very young age of sixteen Ameghino started his own excavations, first near his home town where he detected ancient human bones—a search that he later continued over the entire province of Buenos Aires, including, among other places, in Hermosilla near Bahía Blanca. Based on these findings, he claimed to have identified the bones of what he called *Homo pampeanus*, apparently in the same tertiary strata of the Earth's crust where extinct animals like the *Megatherium* (see Ameghino [1880] 1918) had been found. From this, he concluded that *Homo pampeanus* was a prototype of today's *Homo sapiens* and that these bones were older than any other human skeleton found until then. Thus, according to Ameghino, humankind must have evolved as an autochthonous species in South America, without any migration from Africa or Asia.

Even if Ameghino's theory of a South American autochthony of the human species soon turned out to be entirely erroneous, it provides evidence for a revealing superposition of time scales: Ameghino projects the time scale of the history of humankind upon the national history of the "young" Argentine nation, and he uses his hypothesis of *Homo pampeanus* in order to supplement the short time span since the beginning of the Argentine nation.

But what is at least as important for later, alternative histories of deep time in Argentina is the fact that the pampa in Ameghino has ceased to be just a flat surface in geographic space but has become a layer, or stratum, in the "vertical" history of the Earth. In his biostratigraphy (see fig. 3), which was modified and elaborated on in greater detail in his subsequent research (see Tonni 2011), Ameghino uses the adjective "pampeano" to refer to the tertiary formation where he believes he has discovered human fossil bones. In his research, it is no longer geography but geology that is now the starting point for foundational fictions of the Argentine nation.

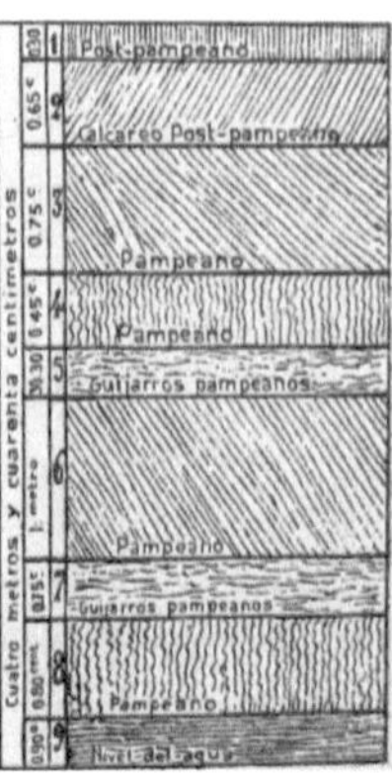

[Fig. 3] Florentino Ameghino's biostratigraphic chart (Source: Ameghino [1880] 1918, vol. 2, s.p., table XVII.)

From here, I will finally turn to another stratum in my trip through space and time that will lead us into the Anthropocene—or at least to its threshold. In terms of Ameghino's biostratigraphy I will now deal with the "post-pampean" formation, which is the formation in direct contact with the surface of the Earth and also where human agency progressively emerges as an active force that contributes to the present changes in stratigraphy. In dealing with this zone, I will turn away from the shores of Argentine rivers or the Atlantic Ocean and enter the muddy transition zone between water and land not very far from the Rio Luján, where Ameghino started his research, i.e., in the delta of the Río de La Plata.

IV. Delta of the Río de La Plata, in the Near Future

As a complement to the conquest of the vast desert of the pampa as the commonplace founding fiction of the Argentine nation, there is a less well-known foundational discourse of Argentine modernity that comes not from the land but from the water. Curiously enough, the first to invent this alternative history is the same person who also invented the "desert fiction," namely Domingo Faustino Sarmiento, in his short essays about the river delta, titled *Carapachay*. These do not deal with the pampa as a desert but instead with the delta of the La Plata river as a starting point for an alternative model of a civilizing process.[6]

What distinguishes this "aquatic" from a "terrestrian" model of civilization in Sarmiento, as well as in other writers who have adopted his model, is the fact that, contrary to the conception of the pampa as a desert that has to be civilized and fertilized entirely by human means, the river delta is in some way an autopoietic landscape in which human beings take advantage of its productivity and its fertility but are not themselves the origin of these dynamics. To express this, Sarmiento establishes an analogy in his introductory essay to the collection *Carapachay*, entitled "Formación. Tradiciones. Tiempos heroicos" (Formation, traditions, heroic times; Sarmiento [1913] 2011, 51–59), with the seven days of creation in the Old Testament—with the crucial difference that in his account the river delta needs no active God to make the Earth emerge from the waters: the active force at work here is none other than sedimentation in the brown waters of the delta, where tons of alluvium arrive with the two rivers Paraná and Uruguay.

6 The river delta is also the setting for another essay by Sarmiento with the title *Argirópolis* (Sarmiento [1850] 2012), in which, adopting the model of Thomas More's *Utopia*, Sarmiento describes a small island in the river delta, named Martín García, as the capital of a future confederation of Latin American states.

I cannot deal here with the political implication of Sarmiento's alternative founding fiction, in which he promotes less a sovereign territorial state (as in his essay on the pampa) than a model of transnational liberal economy, where transport infrastructure only strengthens what he calls "el bello ideal de la viabilidad" (the natural ideal of viability; Sarmiento [1913] 2011, 61) present in the river delta from the very beginning (see Dünne 2020). What is crucial for the alternative scenario of foundational fictions I would like to describe here is the fact that in the river delta two normally incompatible timescales interfere—the scale of human observation and the scale of geological transformation—because of the increased speed with which territories are formed and transformed in this particular landscape.

In his essay *El río sin orillas* (The boundless river; Saer [1991] 2011), one of the major Argentine writers of fluvial literature in the twentieth century, Juan José Saer, describes how, in observing the same spot by the river over several years, he is present at the birth of an island near the shore of the Paraná, which is precisely the river transporting its load of sediment to the delta of the Río de la Plata:

> Desde las barrancas de Paraná que dominan el río, la mirada abarca un horizonte desmedido, hecho casi exclusivamente de islas y de agua. De esas islas aluvionales, una bien enfrente de la costanera, en medio del río, de unos doscientos metros de extensión, es fina y alargada .... De esa isla podría decir, con la misma nostalgia con que un señor ya mayor dice de una hermosa muchacha que de chica supo tenerla sobre las rodillas, que asistí a su nacimiento. (Saer [1991] 2011, 230)

> From the cliffs of Paraná high above the river, the view encompasses an immense horizon, consisting almost exclusively of water and islands. One of these alluvial islands opposite the riverbank in the middle of the river, with an extension of about two hundred meters, is slim and

> elongated. Of this island, I could say that I was present at its birth, with the nostalgia of an elderly man talking about a beautiful young woman that he used to hold on his knees when she was a little girl.

At the end of his detailed description, where he compares himself self-ironically to an elderly man seeing a young girl grow up, Saer speaks, much like Sarmiento, of an island cosmogony from the "magma barroso" (muddy magma; Saer [1991] 2011, 231) of the fluvial sediment. Thus, Saer describes the island as an entity spreading not only in space but also in time:

> A decir verdad, esa isla estaba hecha no únicamente de materia sino también de tiempo acumulado, de la unidad indestructible de tiempo y materia." (Saer [1991] 2011, 231)
>
> To tell the truth, this island was not only made of matter but also of an accumulation of time, of the indestructible unity of time and matter.

Thus, the riverscape in Saer, as in Sarmiento, stands for a stratification of geologic time that becomes observable by humans. But Saer still attributes the forces that lead to the creation and transformation of sedimentary landscapes to "algunas leyes físicas y biológicas universales" (some universal laws of physics and biology; Saer [1991] 2011, 232). In his eyes, riverscapes lend shape to an ontological thinking reaching back to the origins of the philosophy of becoming since Heraclitus and the Presocratics. His fluvial cosmogony takes us to the threshold of a present-day conception of riverscapes that not only expresses the laws of natural becoming but also leads us to question of what is "natural" and what is "cultural" in the Anthropocene.

According to recent research, rivers can be regarded as emblematic for the Anthropocenic condition of present times since, in riverscapes, the question of human impact on the surface of the Earth can no longer be distinguished from a "prehuman" nature. River deltas all over the world, with their mostly dense populations, are thus not only places where geological time accumulates so that this accumulation can be observed from a human perspective, but also places where different timescales and temporalities interfere. In the huge river deltas all over the planet, the global condition of life in the Anthropocene becomes legible at a local scale (see Haus der Kulturen der Welt 2019, and Kelly 2018). Amitav Ghosh alludes to this in his essay about climate change and the literary imagination, mentioned above, when he refers to new communities of experience between the inhabitants of the river deltas all over the Earth:

> But the Earth of the Anthropocene is precisely a world of insistent, inescapable continuities, animated by forces that are nothing if not inconceivably vast .... No less than they mock the discontinuities and boundaries of the nation-state do these connections defy the boundedness of "place," creating communities of experience between Bengal and Louisiana, New York and Mumbai, Tibet and Alaska. (Ghosh 2016, 61)

The delta of the Río de la Plata is certainly part of this connected history. The sites of this history may be no less important in terms of a new literary imagination building a bridge between the narrative reconstitution of scenes from deep time in the past and an imagination of possible Anthropocenic futures. One might even argue, following Eva Horn (2014), that a temporal perspective toward the future is necessarily implied in the imagination of the Anthropocene: according to Horn, thinking about the Anthropocene presupposes the necessity of imagining the Earth after the end of the human presence on the planet, of assuming a state of life on Earth "without us" (as a species-we).

To conclude with an example of such literary scenarios of Anthropocene rivers in the near future, where human life on Earth is not yet over but seriously threatened, I would like to turn to two novels by the Argentine writer Claudia Aboaf: *El rey del agua* (*The Water King*, Aboaf 2016) and *El ojo y la flor* (*The Eye and the Flower*, Aboaf 2019).[7] What is interesting in these novels is less the story of the two sisters Andrea and Juana who, after being separated for several years, finally find their way back to each other at the end of the trilogy. This rather traditional plot in a Lotmanian sense is, one might say, only the pretense for a curious intermingling of human-scale issues with environmental transformations of the river delta in the near future.

The dystopian plot of these novels is based on the assumption that the river delta becomes one of the richest places in a world at a moment of global history when nation states are abandoned in favor of small *polis*-like states centered around single towns—in this case, the largest town of the delta of the Río de la Plata, called Tigre. The ruler of this small state, who is called "Tempe"[8] and is described as the "water king" alluded to in the title, has made a fortune by selling huge quantities of water to the rest of the planet, where drinking water has become scarce due to a scenario of climate change that is not described in greater detail. But after a short period of exploiting the water resources of the Río de la Plata and its huge drainage basin, the delta starts to dry up and is slowly being transformed into a landscape of deep mud.

What is so remarkable about this transformation of the river delta is not only the fact that the dystopian fiction of Claudia Aboaf can be read as a "narrative of prevention," as Eva Horn (2014, 297ff.) has put it, i.e., as a scenario of a possible future that is told precisely because it should not happen in the real world. But moreover, even as they develop a scenario for the future, they also constitute a complex literary archive of references to

7 These two novels form a trilogy together with *Pichonas* (*Little Doves*, 2014). I would like to express my gratitude to the Argentine writer and seafarer Juan Bautista Duizeide, who introduced me to these novels.

8 This name is an allusion to a text by Marcos Sastre, who was the author of one of the first literary descriptions of the delta, published in 1858 (Sastre 2005).

Argentinean fluvial literature from the nineteenth century to the present. This interpenetration of past and future is twofold: it is intertextual and it can be seen, as well, in the materiality of the fictional world. The future scenario of a receding water level eventually makes visible what had been accumulated in the sediments of the delta throughout history. For instance, the father of the two heroines is one of the people who "disappeared" (or who were made to disappear) not much earlier, during what the book identifies only as some military dictatorship, by being drowned at the Iguazú waterfalls; the "water king," who constantly analyzes the quality of the drinking water he sells, pretends he has detected a trace of the father's DNA in the water of the river delta.

Here, I would like to refer to the last paragraph of the *El Rey del agua*, the second part of the trilogy, where Andrea goes through a kind of birth scene while swimming in the waters of the river delta: she is born (or reborn) into a water that not only announces a new life but is already polluted by half-dissolved corpses that slightly touch her leg while floating by (among these corpses might be that of her own father):

> Alcanza la desembocadura. Con una brazada ingresa a la volute formada por el encuentro entre corrientes. Gira impulsada en el remolina de agua, nada nada como criatura nueva. Algo le roza una pierna. No se altera. Nada en el río vivo, entre los Muertos disueltos en el agua (Aboaf 2016, 141).
>
> She reaches the mouth of the river. With a stroke she enters into the swirl produced by the encounter of the currents. She turns around in the water vortex, swimming, swimming like a new creature. Something brushes against her leg. She is not unsettled. She swims in the living river in the midst of the dead dissolved in the water.

And in the final part of the trilogy, when the water level falls, the first bones to appear on the shores of the Río de la Plata, near the industrial site of Ensenada further down the delta in a highly polluted zone, are those of what might be a dog—followed by many more bones that now seem to be human:

> A medio metro debajo del nivel costero, ven los huesos de lo que podría ser un perro. La calavera cerrada por los colmillos fieros, entrecruzados, prensada entre capas de sedimentos. Alguno enterró a su compañero sin calcular que quedaría expuesto. La respiración se les hace más profunda. Se alejan del borde: esa franja blanca continúa después del perro, parece también ser un osario de personas muertas. (Aboaf 2019, 128)

> Half a meter below the coastline, they see the bones of what might be a dog. The skull closed with its fierce, interlaced crossed fangs, pressed together between layers of sediments. Someone had buried his companion without realizing that it might be exposed. Their breath grows deeper. They move away from the shore. That white strip continues beyond the dog, and appears also to be an ossuary of dead people.

Hence, curiously, this dystopian fiction of a nearby Anthropocenic future of the riverscape of the Río de la Plata also contains a landscape of memory that refers to the factual history of the Argentine nation. Imagining a future scenario of "slow" environmental violence (see Nixon 2011) at a geological scale seems inseparable from political acts of violence in the nearby past, especially in Argentina, where the allusion to the "desaparecidos" (the "missing" people who disappeared during the last military dictatorship) is all too clear.

***

It can be concluded that the bones found in the "post-pampean" sediments of the Río de la Plata in Claudia Aboaf's novel are no longer there to serve as new ground for a "foundational fiction" in deep time, as in, for instance, Ameghino's case of *Homo pampeanus*; rather, they may be described as "unfounding" fictions.[9] This not only gives us a literary account of the precarious interaction of environmental, economic, and sociopolitical processes in the Anthropocene for which riverscapes are somewhat emblematic. The unfounding fictions of Aboaf also invent complex ways of articulating different temporalities: this complex way of articulating different timescales can be a specific quality of literary fictions, distinguishing them from other ways of configuring the complexity of Anthropocenic processes in terms of their material and semiotic aspects.[10] So at least in terms of literary imagination, and contrary to what Amitav Ghosh thinks, the "Great Derangement" of the Anthropocene might be quite a productive crisis.

References

Aboaf, Claudia. 2016. *El rey del agua*. Buenos Aires: Alfaguara.

Aboaf, Claudia. 2019. *El ojo y la flor*. Buenos Aires: Alfaguara.

Ameghino, Florentino. (1880) 1918. *La antigüedad del hombre en el Plata*. 2 vols, edited by Alfredo J. Torcelli. Buenos Aires: La Cultura Argentina.

Anthropocene Working Group. 2019. *Subcommission on Quaternary Stratigraphy*. Accessed March 10, 2020. http://quaternary.stratigraphy.org/working-groups/anthropocene/.

Balzac, Honoré de. (1831) 1974. *La peau de chagrin*, edited by Sylvestre de Sacy. Paris: Gallimard folio.

Balzac, Honoré de. 1888. *The Magic Skin*, translated by Katherine Wormeley. London: Routledge.

Braudel, Fernand. 1958. "Histoire et sciences sociales: La longue durée." *Annales* 13: 725–53.

Chakrabarty, Dipesh. 2009. "The Climate of History: Four Theses." *Critical Inquiry* 35: 197–222.

Chakrabarty, Dipesh. 2012. "Postcolonial Studies and the Challenge of Climate Change." *New Literary History* 43: 1–18.

9 The expression "unfounding" echoes the notion "effondement," a neologism invented by Gilles Deleuze (1969, 303ff.) as a superposition of "foundation" (*fondement*) and "collapse" (*effondrement*).

10 Regarding "narratives of the Anthropocene," see Gabriele Dürbeck (2018), whose approach differs from mine inasmuch she is more interested in social metanarratives of the present moment than in their literary genealogy. For a similar approach from a Latin American perspective, see Svampa (2018).

Clark, Timothy. 2015. *Ecocriticism on the Edge: The Anthropocene as a Threshold Concept*. London: Bloomsbury.

Crutzen, Paul J. 2002. "Ecology of Mankind." *Nature* 415: 23.

Cuvier, Georges. (1825) 1969. *Discours sur les révolutions de la surface du globe: et sur les changemens qu'elles ont produits dans le règne animal*. Bruxelles: Culture et Civilisation.

Cuvier, Georges. 1804. "Sur le Megatherium: autre animal de la famille des Paresseux, mais de la taille du Rhinoceros dont un squelette fossile presque complet est conservé au cabinet royal d'histoire naturelle à Madrid." *Annales du Museum National d'Histoire Naturelle* 4 (29): 376–387.

De Iuliis, Gerardo, et al. 2005. "El legado del megaterio." *Museo* 3 (19): 33–38.

De Landa, Manuel. 1997. *A Thousand Years of Nonlinear History*. New York: Swerve.

Deleuze, Gilles. 1969. *Logique du sens*. Paris: Minuit.

Descola, Philippe. 2013. *Beyond Nature and Culture*. Chicago: University of Chicago Press.

Dünne, Jörg. 2016. *Die katastrophische Feerie: Geologie, Spektakularität und Historizität in der französischen Erzählliteratur der Moderne*. Konstanz: Konstanz University Press.

Dünne, Jörg. 2020. "Cultural Techniques and Founding Fictions." In *Cultural Techniques. Assembling Spaces, Texts & Collectives*, edited by Jörg Dünne, Kathrin Fehringer, Kristina Kuhn, and Wolfgang Struck, 47–59. Berlin: De Gruyter.

Dünne, Jörg. 2020a "Escribiendo el "tiempo profundo": Ficciones fundacionales y el Antropoceno." *Orbis tertius* 25 (31). https://doi.org/10.24215/18517811e146.

Dürbeck, Gabriele. 2018. "Narrative des Anthropozän: Systematisierung eines interdisziplinären Diskurses." *Kulturwissenschaftliche Zeitschrift* 3 (1): 1–20.

Ghosh, Amitav. 2016. *The Great Derangement: Climate Change and the Unthinkable*. Chicago: Chicago University Press.

Gould, Stephen Jay. 1987. *Time's Arrow, Time's Cycle: Myth and Metaphor in the Discovery of Geological Time*. Cambridge: Harvard University Press.

Haraway, Donna J. 2016. *Staying with the Trouble: Making Kin in the Chthulucene*. Durham, NC: Duke University Press.

Haus der Kulturen der Welt. 2019. "Mississippi: An Anthropocene River." Accessed March 10, 2020. https://anthropocene-curriculum.org/.

Horn, Eva. 2014. *Zukunft als Katastrophe*. Frankfurt a.M.: Fischer.

Kelly, Jason M., Philip Scarpino, Helen Berry, James Syvitski, and Michel Meybeck, eds. 2018. *Rivers of the Anthropocene*. Oakland: University of California Press.

Koselleck, Reinhart. 2000. *Zeitschichten: Studien zur Historik*. Frankfurt a.M.: Suhrkamp.

Latour, Bruno. 2017. *Facing Gaia: Eight Lectures on the New Climatic Regime*. Translated by Cathy Porter. Cambridge and Malden, MA: Polity Press.

Lorimer, Jamie. 2017. "The Anthropo-Scene: A Guide for the Perplexed." *Social Studies of Science* 47 (1): 117–42.

Lotman, Jurij M. 1977. *The Structure of the Artistic Text*. Ann Arbor: University of Michigan.

Moore, Jason W., ed. 2016. *Anthropocene or Capitalocene? Nature, History, and the Crisis of Capitalism*. Oakland: PM Press.

Nixon, Rob. 2011. *Slow Violence and the Environmentalism of the Poor*. Cambridge: Harvard University Press.

Podgorny, Irina. 2009. *El sendero del tiempo y de las causas accidentales: Los espacios de la prehistoria en la Argentina, 1850–1910*. Rosario: Prohistoria.

Podgorny, Irina. 2015. "Human Origins in the New World? Florentino Ameghino and the Emergence of Prehistoric Archaeology in the Americas (1875–1912)." *Paleo-America* 1 (1): 68–90.

Rodríguez, Fermín. 2010. *Un desierto para la nación: la escritura del vacío*. Buenos Aires: Eterna Cadencia.

Rudwick, Martin. 2005. *Bursting the Limits of Time: The Reconstruction of Geohistory in the Age of Revolution*. Chicago: University of Chicago Press.

Rudwick, Martin. 2008: *Worlds before Adam: The Reconstruction of Geohistory in the Age of Reform*. Chicago: University of Chicago Press.

Saer, Juan José. (1991) 2011. *El río sin orillas*. Buenos Aires: Seix Barral.

Sarmiento, Domingo Faustino. (1845) 2004. *Facundo*. Buenos Aires: Agebe.

Sarmiento, Domingo Faustino. (1913) 2011. *El Carapachay*. Buenos Aires: Eudeba.

Sarmiento, Domingo Faustino. (1850) 2012. *Argirópolis*. Villa María: EDUVIM.

Sastre, Marcos. (1858) 2005. *El Tempe argentino*, edited by Carlos Bernatek. Buenos Aires: Biblioteca Nacional/Colihue.

Stockhammer, Robert. 2017. "Philology in the Anthropocene." *Yearbook of Research in English and American Literature* 33: 43–64.

Svampa, Maristela. 2018. "Imágenes del fin: Narrativas de la crisis socioecológica en el Antropoceno." *Nueva Sociedad* 278. Accessed March 10, 2020. https://nuso.org/articulo/svampa-crisis-ecologica-antropoceno-calentamiento-global/.

Tonni, Eduardo P. 2011. "Ameghino y la estratigrafía pampeana un siglo después." *Asociación Paleontológica Argentina* 12 (1): *Vida y obra de Florentino Ameghino*: 69–79.

Yusoff, Kathryn. 2018. *A Billion Black Anthropocenes or None*. Minneapolis: University of Minnesota Press.

Zalasiewicz, Jan, Colin N. Waters, Mark Williams, and Colin P. Summerhayes, eds. 2019. *The Anthropocene as a Geological Time Unit: A Guide to the Scientific Evidence and Current Debate*. Cambridge: Cambridge University Press.

Tectony

Kinga Tóth

Patch the craters with yarn dipped in clay, darn with yarn dipped in oil. Earthquake rockfall fissure drainage, greater burdock leaves green receptors dampen the clods of earth, wet the stone slabs. The continents separate again, migratory birds circle above, the dance carves new continents, prehistoric reptiles plop their eggs between the stones, the waters of the seas are warmed. The coastal vegetable growers of reform farming bind contract with herbs, no more cattle stomachs in turtles, we retch up grassballs grasshypae when we clear ourselves, we roll soap nuts onto our appendices, sprinkle them with ferns, collect the air, cook the fungus down to a medicinal solution and dream fruit. We return our organs to the earth, so a new seed can be produced in our two palms.

Translated by Owen Good

EPISTEMOLOGY

ECOLOGY

DECOLONIALITY

ANTHROPOCENE

CYBERNETICS

LIQUEFACTION

[4]

Genealogical Liquefaction: Epistemic Formations of the Anthropocene

Jakob Claus

Assuming the Anthropocene marks an epistemological fault line that liquefies and questions traditional forms of knowledge, this text argues for a detailed analysis of two of its possible genealogies. It firstly follows a turn to ecology via environmentality and the offsets of cybernetics, thereby proposing that a general ecology itself marks a current epistemic formation. In contrast, a critical genealogy of the Anthropocene's colonial condition points at coloniality as the unthought but constitutive momentum for the modern episteme. Thus, both genealogies outline a specific understanding of modernity leading to the shifts at stake, and suggest possibilities to navigate these unsettled conditions.

When oil spills, Earth opens its archives.
Tom McCarthy

The critical writing of history is a continuous struggle to liberate the past from within the unconscious of a collective that forgets the conditions of its own existence.
Susan Buck-Morss

In geology, liquefaction refers to the "becoming-liquid" of a terrestrial surface due to tectonic activity: low-lying water is pressed upwards and liquefies formerly solid layers. The Earth's surface floats as a floe on aqueous subsoil. At the same time, the term implies any material and physical process of liquefaction, for example the phase transition from gaseous or solid to liquid. The image of soil liquefaction plays with the simultaneity of these states, a certain indecision, and its temporary limitation. If clods of earth slide over each other, drift apart, or disappear entirely for a time, a previously calm and "reliable" landscape moves and reassembles. Liquefaction implies geological rearrangement and emergence—processual landscapes. It is then not only due to linguistic parallels a metaphor for epistemic dynamics, often referred to in terms such as fracture, discontinuity, emergence, or deposition. Thus, the Anthropocene might be understood as an epistemological fault line with various points of friction or hypocenters, from which sedimented knowledge is liquefied.

In seismology, a hypocenter describes the seismic source of tectonic activity located vertically below the epicenter and along a fault line. Hypocenters are therefore mainly identified by seismographs via epicenters that can be measured and located on the Earth's surface. The slow and continuous movements of a fault line thus might only be mapped indirectly by observing epicenters. The Anthropocene in this regard is neither a single locus nor an event, but a continuous and winding fault line that can be traced along discourses on epochal ruptures, the climate crisis, buried historicity and narratives, ecological devastation, critical epistemologies, or simply the crisis of future life on the planet. Only what previously seemed solid can liquefy—what has been displaced and forgotten in geological depth streams up into the realm of the visible and utterable. In its sudden appearance on the surface, however, the emerged resists immediate and unambiguous description, although various tendencies and patterns are recognizable in the strata as elements of a displaced past.

Following this vague restlessness, I depart from the assumption that the Anthropocene marks an epistemological fault line. The current re-formation of knowledge represents an opportunity to open up relations between perspectives and questions previously submerged. But from which standpoint might the moving surface be described and mapped, and what would be the possible consequences? The intention is to focus on two hypocenters that propose a critical history of structures and formations of knowledge and provide approaches for the turbulent and comprehensive epicenters of globality and agency in the Anthropocene. Firstly, I refer to the genealogy of the concept of ecology, which, gaining its momentum from cybernetics and media technological developments in the twentieth century, makes visible a fundamental ecologization. Secondly, I follow crucial arguments of decolonial theory and its criticism of modernity's paradigm of knowledge and cognition—highlighting its persistent colonial constitution. Both genealogies refer to and propose different historical perspectives in the present provoked by the Anthropocene discourse. Therefore, what follows is an examination of (de-)coloniality and ecology as forms of knowledge and possible ways to map the epistemological implications of the Anthropocene on different layers.

[Fig. 1] Liquid soil and dust at the beginning of a dream sequence in the "Zone" in Andrei Tarkovsky's *Stalker*. (Still from *4 Waters: Deep Implicancy*, Denise Ferreira da Silva and Arjuna Neuman, 2018, courtesy of the artists)

The Anthropocene as an extensive fault line refers to possible pasts and futures twofold. It thus calls for a genealogical and historical location and the attempt is to explain its emergence, but at the same time to raise questions of concomitant epistemological effects and formations of knowledge. Following Michel Foucault's conception of genealogy, the emphasis is on the relations of forces and emergence and how "these forces wage against each other or against adverse circumstance" (Foucault 1996, 149). But genealogy as a history of configurations can only offer an "impure" narrative and a partial cartography of knowledge (Sarasin et al. 2007, 13–14).[1] In this sense, geographer Kathryn

1 "Genealogies are fundamentally 'impure' – they are stories that tell of complicated circumstances and multiple origins, in which scientific and everyday knowledge interpenetrate, in which original intentions are turned into the opposite and scientific knowledge only becomes what was supposedly sought from the very beginning at the very end of a research process itself. … Precisely at this point, however … it must turn into a *history of knowledge*" (Sarasin et al. 2007, 13–14; my translation).

Yusoff characterizes the task of critical genealogy as the questioning of the sediments involved and the basal entanglement of power and knowledge.

> The first step in such a genealogy of knowledge production is to address the processes of subjectification ...: specifically, to see what modes of subjectification make it possible for a subject (Anthropos) to become an object of possible knowledge (Anthropocene). (Yusoff 2015, 7)

What then becomes evident is that origin stories are designated leverage points in order to highlight and deconstruct their historical emergence and current effects. Both perspectives explicitly address this logic as it is essential not only for the epistemo-technological trajectory of cybernetics and ecology but also for a decolonial deconstruction of hegemonic knowledge structures.

Omnipresent Ecologies

As the French collective Tiqqun claims, since the middle of the twentieth century cybernetics has become the dominant technological principle, political narrative, and thus rationality of government. From their perspective "[t]he *cybernetic hypothesis* ... has definitively supplanted the liberal hypothesis. Unlike the latter, it would have us think of biological, physical, and social behaviors as being integrally programmed and reprogrammable" (Tiqqun 2020, 25). As the thinking of communication and control and the knowledge about regulation and feedback, cybernetics is framed as fable or myth in the sense of providing a universal horizon of meaning and approach to the world as system. To conceive cybernetics as a historical phase yet also as a proliferating narrative is what could be referred to as "cybernetic episteme" (Pias 2004, 15; my translation). It not only includes the military-scientific complex after the Second World War and during the Cold War, the hope for a universal science, a mode of rationality and governmentality as analyzed by Foucault, but also an epistemological formation expanding to what philosopher Erich Hörl (2017) characterizes as the process of "general ecologization" and subsequently as technoecological condition.[2] This condition evolved via cybernetics and the logic of environmentality to become a basal description of (post-)modernity's fascination with technology. In contrast to coloniality as the suppressed condition of the modern episteme, "the question of technology" functions as the central and thereby consciously prominent condition. According to philosopher Yuk Hui, diagnosing Anthropocene ruptures from the perspective of technology implies a specific "cosmotechnical" constitution addressing the reciprocal dependence of technological evolution and its corresponding cosmologies: "[I]t means," as he writes, "the unification of the cosmic order and moral order through technical activities. Human activities, which are always accompanied by technical objects ... are in this sense always cosmotechnical" (Hui 2017, 4). The entanglement of environmental media-technologies, the concept of ecology and the diagnosis of a fundamental epistemic shift fueled by technology allow for a first measurement of the Anthropocene fault line.

The trajectory of cybernetization, broadly summarized, appears as a history of rationalism and variance of the phantasm of total organization, management, and governance. Thus, cybernetics has been predestined to be a sole and universal tool to steer and control societal dynamics and psychological structures of desire. It became an epistemological utopia as it insisted among other axioms on a definition of information and communication freed from all materiality, that is to say circulating without resistance. Control and management of information flows and behavior and,

2 Hörl diagnoses the process of ecologization and the "great environmental switch" as an emerging and fundamental transformation in the history of sense (Hörl 2018; Hörl 2017, 14). In earlier publications he mainly developed the concept of the technological condition, putting more emphasis especially on technology and environmentality but not ecology itself (see Hörl 2011).

in conjunction with this, noise or uncertainty, remain nevertheless the basic principles, as Tiqqun asserts:

> As a body of knowledge, it [cybernetics] brings together a set of heterogeneous discourses that all address the *practical problem of mastering uncertainty*. What they express fundamentally, in their various domains of application, is the desire for an order to be restored and, further, that it have [sic] the stability to endure. (Tiqqun 2020, 38)

Cybernetics' principle of control and feedback loops aims at insecurity, never diminishing it completely, but integrating it into the system's own loops and thus making it a productive—or manageable—uncertainty. If any signal carries meaning, noise is not only a distractive or disruptive factor but has always been information itself. As the scholar in literature and science Bruce Clarke notes, "if noise is *also* information ... then the concept of information incorporates the unity of the difference between signal and noise. Signal *or* noise, it's all information" (Clarke 2010, 166). Every system then is conceptualized with its corresponding environment that is not conceived as irritation but as its co-constitutive element. They are in constant exchange, recursive interaction, and an adaptive relation. Environment and system are not separable on a material or conceptual level but interact reciprocally.[3] Deviation and uncertainty become manageable productivity factors—the unforeseen is both problem and potential for the cybernetic episteme. "Stubbornness and deviation ... become productive, as they serve to produce ever new, unexpected challenges to adaptation" (Pias 2004, 29; my translation).

Starting from this premise, Hörl's thesis of a contemporary epistemological shift concentrates on the concept of ecology that evolved out of cybernetics' grasp of environments. It divides into "restricted ecologies" as forms of capture, capitalist

3 For a recent and extensive discussion of cybernetics' application of recursivity and control of environments see Sprenger 2019, 204–22.

extraction and restricting power/knowledge complexes on the one side, and on the other a mode of thinking relations and the becoming environmental of sense itself in what he calls "general ecology" (Hörl 2017). Closed ecologies, in contrast, have been characterized by the "holistic and integrative" (Golley 1993, 8) concept of ecosystems that generalizes organisms and their environments as a universal organization principle. The concept forms an intersection of biology and the notion of complex systems as ever-adapting informational structures. As Clarke puts it, "the cybernetic development of the ecosystem concept brings ecology directly into the systems-theoretical treatment of system-environment relations" (2014, 142). The botanist and ecologist Alfred Tansley, who introduced the term in 1935, described it as "the basic units of nature," thus ranging "from the universe as a whole down to the atom" (as cited in Golley 1993, 8). But what becomes evident in, for example, literary theorist Elisabeth DeLoughrey's analysis of US nuclear tests from the 1940s onwards, is the narrative, cosmotechnical, and epistemic implications of ecosystems and restricted ecologies. She outlines how a specific systems-thinking evolved around these tests that ranges from cybernetics as knowledge of war to the conceptualization of ecologies as discrete, closed and observable systems, leading to the emergence of ecology as an independent discipline. "The ecosystem blurred the distinction between inorganic and organic by reducing everything to energy as the common denominator. Nature had become a system of components that could be managed, manipulated, and controlled" (Greg Mitman as cited in DeLoughrey 2013, 173). The Pacific Islands, where many of the early US nuclear tests took place, were considered "neutral" closed ecologies within which the exchange of energy and information could be perfectly traced and manipulated. DeLoughrey points towards the inherent colonial "myth of isolates" that regards milieus as *terra nullius*, merely abstract territory, thereby negating the differences between the islands as geological formations and the Indigenous inhabitants: "The concept of the closed system or isolate was tied closely to the colonization of islands and rendering them into nuclear laboratories" (DeLoughrey 2013, 172). Closed ecologies hence not only informed knowledge production at the time but are themselves expressions of a cybernetically informed episteme.

But if the Pacific Islands are defined as an ecosystem, then their environment is also an ecosystem, which in turn is embedded in an environment until finally the biosphere and the planet itself appear as ecosystems. This becomes explicitly evident with the Gaia hypothesis formulated by Lynn Margulis and James Lovelock in the 1970s (Lovelock and Margulis 1974). From a systems theory perspective, Margulis and Lovelock conceived of Earth as an organism that recursively regulates itself (and organic life) via interdependence and feedback loops. The Gaia hypothesis appears thus as continuation of Tansley's frictionless scalable concept of ecosystems on a planetary level, obeying a logic of totality.[4]

Accordingly, unrestricted ecology proposes an understanding of environmentality that in fact itself has no conceptual outside, "no outside outside the environment" (Sprenger 2019, 370; my translation). The "disappearance of the outside" implies an ecology without ecology or an "ecology without nature" (Morton 2009). But this disappearance in the historical context of the Apollo missions also implies a universal perspective that assumed itself to be natural, thereby being heavily influenced by the cybernetic claim of universal applicability. What cybernetics' insisting on a general organizational principle implies becomes apparent in geographer Denis Cosgrove's term of the *Apollonian gaze*. If the planet emerges as a cybernetic organism, the human ascends to become its omnipotent navigator: "The Apollonian gaze, which

4 For a discussion on the recent re-emergence of the Gaia hypothesis and its implications see Friedrich et al. 2018. Furthermore, Clarke argues for a detailed understanding of the systems theoretical conception of globality that is not to be confused with totality of systems (Clarke 2017, 5).

 pulls diverse life on Earth into a vision of unity, is individualized, a divine and mastering view from a single perspective" (Cosgrove 2001, xi). For Spaceship Earth as a steerable vehicle is almost a paradigmatic expression of cybernetics' longing for globality, which promises to capture any context at any scale: "The idea of seeing the globe seems also to induce desires of ordering and controlling the object of vision" (Cosgrove 2001, 5).

The Anthropocene fault line appears as an unwittingly entered rupture yet simultaneously as a continuation of cybernetics' whole Earth perspective, systematically extended towards planetary and conceptual totality originating from colonial systems. As Yusoff (2017) suggests: "The origin of the desire for real-time globality and telepresent communications is already evident in the colonial networks of Empire—the telecommunication and transportation networks powered by coal and before coal by slavery." Hui subsequently identifies the central problem of the Anthropocene as a globalized and thereby naturalized cosmological order and a "gigantic cybernetic system in the process of realization" (Hui 2017, 2). Globality here emerges as a structural moment and radiating epicenter.

Hörl's notion of a "general ecology" however hints at a slightly different direction as it summarizes the discourse of cybernetics, biology, and systems theory and assumes that ecology itself has become the principle of an epistemological hypocenter. General ecology then not only outlines environmentality as today's primary mode of worlding as cybernetics' afterlife in decentralized control, governmentality and a specific power/knowledge complex, but moreover as an ecological mode of thinking and speculative form of critique: "General ecology is the title of a thinking of becoming-environmental that proceeds in terms of a formal analysis of environmentality" (Hörl 2018, 157). Consequently, the brief history of ecology shows its characteristics as a hypocenter that manifests in principles of environment, globality and control as signatures of the "Anthropocene-in-the-making" (Yusoff 2018, 25).

Re-Narrating Origins

In her book *A Billion Black Anthropocenes or None* (2018) Yusoff examines the narrative structures and colonial logics of the Anthropocene discourse. She claims that questions of origin and histories can and must be re-negotiated in the light of the Anthropocene as epistemological liquefaction particularly unearths its conditions of origin. These manifest as "enforced intimacy" (Yusoff 2018, xii) between Blackness and the inhuman, forming geography's imperial and extractive dispositifs of subjectivity and resources. She interprets the Anthropocene as a paradigm which, on the one hand, is legitimized by knowledge of geography—itself a genuinely modern science—and, on the other hand, proves to be a "descriptive statement" of present colonial conditions. Due to its global character, knowledge about and in the Anthropocene, she argues, is constitutively dependent on the mode and the perspective from which history is written and is in consequence often a continuation of coloniality. Referring to philosopher Sylvia Wynter's concept of the descriptive statement, Yusoff emphasizes that decolonial genealogies deconstruct seemingly unalterable narratives a society tells about itself.[5] By highlighting the recursive and somehow autopoietic logic of a society's reference system Wynter offers an approach to modernity's colonial self-portrayal. It implies that what is recognized as a possible and legitimate mode of being human, knowledge and the origin story are intrinsically part of this same hegemonic formation (Wynter 2003). Ultimately, with the descriptive statement, Wynter aims at a logic inscribed in a world view and order that depicts the unreflective self-conception of a society, which, for this very reason, is perceived as ahistorical truth. It thus becomes a pivotal point of any epistemic order. The concept exposes the moment of reflexivity and recursivity—i.e., uncovering the constructedness of a self-portrait imagined

5 Wynter herself borrows the term from the anthropologist and cybernetician Gregory Bateson (Wynter 2015, 210).

as natural and given. She exemplifies this via hegemonic conceptions of modes of being (legitimately) human throughout the last centuries. Thereby Wynter evokes the logic of the human secured as a rational and political being up to the eighteenth century, then superseded in the wake of Darwinian knowledge by an "overrepresentation" of man as purely biological (Wynter 2003, 277–78). Wynter's conclusion is that both modes co-produce their constitutively other in the form of irrationals, slaves, and racialized subjects (Wynter 2003, 264). Coloniality has been the constitutive "unthought"[6] for the modern episteme—that which is excluded from moral and epistemic formations. In contrast to technology and its formation of epistemo-cosmological orders, coloniality has held the position of a secondary and suppressed—precisely unthought—discourse that nevertheless haunts modern European thinking.

However, Yusoff illustrates the social and historical emergence of origin narratives, thereby indicating the colonial constitution of geography and knowledge production that become visible anew. Unsettling epistemic structures would then be a premise to deconstruct the intertwining of hegemonic and unthought histories that negate the intimacy between race and geology (Yusoff 2018, 21). Emphasizing the colonial-capitalist and exploitative foundational history of globalization, Yusoff argues against an innocent description of the present.

> The histories of the Anthropocene unfold a brutal experience for much of the world's racialized poor and without

6 I use the term in reference to the cultural historian and literary scholar Saidiya Hartman, who describes "the slave" as the unthought part of the national order. "On one hand, the slave is the foundation of the national order, and, on the other, the slave occupies the position of the unthought" (Hartman and Wilderson 2003, 184–85). Contrary, literary scholar Katherine Hayles for example deploys the unthought in the context of neuroscience as "nonconscious cognitive processes [...that are] nevertheless essential for consciousness to function" (Hayles 2017, 1). Even though describing a similar logic, she suggests a more affirmative tone of the term in regard to its potentialities for understanding human consciousness.

> due attention to the historicity of those events ...; the Anthropocene simply consolidates power via this innocence in the present. (Yusoff 2018, 11–12)

The imaginary innocent present, she argues, nevertheless requires a conceptual actor to conform to a self-referential origin. The description of man—anthropos—as monolithic actor encompasses humanity and "its" history as a single uniform species. The anthropos marks the emergence of a "new" descriptive statement, positioned as an agent of an epoch and a geological history. Instead of a naturalized matrix of rationality or biology, now geology suggests a pregiven history that ensures its own validity by suppressing the knowledge about its narrative and social construction (Wynter 2003, 325–26). What is left aside then, are the manifold conditions of possibility that made the emergence of the geocentric descriptive statement possible in the first place.

> The social reproduction of 'Man' as a figure and origin for this epoch actively excludes the apprehension of important forms of differentiation and genealogical critique that might be useful in forestalling the continuation of the very conditions that produced this threshold moment. (Yusoff 2015, 8)

This "threshold moment" then manifests as the debate around potential "golden spikes" to pin down the Anthropocene to a definite origin—a fixed point within the liquefied surface. In the debate the universalizing tendencies of the Anthropocene become evident by positioning the Eurocentric perspective as "neutral" and subsequently as "the" global narrative. Concentrating on mainly two contingent dates (around the middle of the twentieth century, the development of nuclear weapons, and the "Great Acceleration" of around 1800 as the dawn of European industrialization and a global capitalist economy) the debate emphasizes measurable and technology-influenced time spans that should serve as solid ground to drive in the golden spike.[7] But what is left aside are the predating dynamics and processes that made these dates possible in the first place. This can be grasped as a continuation of the "epistemic violence" (Davis and Todd 2017, 772) that Heather Davis and Zoe Todd invoke as the inherently colonial logic surrounding narratively constructed origins. Instead of following this trajectory they suggest asking "how rock and climate are bound to flesh" (Davis and Todd 2017, 769) in order to recognize the current ecological crisis as one that is based on the capitalist-colonial logic of "extraction and accumulation through dispossession" (Davis and Todd 2017, 764).

Accordingly, two alternative origins might be considered that reveal the limited and partial perspective of any distinct date. Firstly the "Columbian Exchange" around 1610 makes visible the global exchange of humans, flora and fauna by the transatlantic slave trade (Yusoff 2018, 29–32). It laid the ground for large-scale experiments with plantations in the Americas, conceptualized as *terra nullius*. In reference to Wynter, Yusoff secondly considers the first plantations around 1452 on Madeira as the signature of a globally evolving economy that rested on slavery and forced labor (Yusoff 2018, 33–35). These were built on forced labor and spawned a notion of (frictionless) scalability to economic processes and relations toward natural resources.[8] The arrival of Europeans in the "New World" around 1492 manifested and reinforced the structures of forced labor and large-scale production. The asymmetry between potential origins becomes evident in relation to the question of "who and what is addressed" by each

7 See therefore the affirmative vote of the Anthropocene Working Group about whether the Anthropocene should be treated as a "chronostratigraphic unit defined by a GSSP" (Subcommission on Quaternary Stratigraphy 2019) as well as the exemplary discussion of Global Boundary Stratotype Section and Points for the Anthropocene (Waters et al. 2018).

8 Anna Lowenhaupt Tsing (2012) discusses the aspect of scalability as a foundational principle of capitalist production in regard to its colonial origins on plantations and highlights the vast implications for modernity's concepts of labor and nature.

geological marker. A decolonial genealogy of the Anthropocene discourse necessarily implies material and discursive practices that link it to the material and epistemic violence at its core.

Following Wynter's deconstructive approach to modes of being human, Yusoff summarizes the dialectic of epistemic inclusion and exclusion. "[G]eologic origin stories function as identity politics that coheres around an exclusive notion of humanity (coded white)." Continuing:

> Origins draw borders that define inclusion and exclusion … narrating a line of purpose (read Progress) and purposefulness (read Civilization), while overlooking accident, misdirection, or the shadow geology of disposable lives, waste, toxicity, contamination, extinction, and exhaustion. There is not geology on one hand and stories about geology on the other; rather, there is an axis of power and performance that meets within these geologic objects and the narratives they tell about the human story. (Yusoff 2018, 24)[9]

Coloniality not only represents another hypocenter of the fault line, but also formulates a stance on the Anthropocene's tendency towards universality and globality. As argued in the context of ecology and cybernetics' longing for universality, globality, understood as universal access to the world, is decisive for the Anthropocene's claim. Thus, decolonial genealogy allows to carve out another perspective on globality as a defining aspect of the present epistemic liquefaction.

In her book *Toward a Global Idea of Race* (2007), artist and theorist Denise Ferreira da Silva suggests the term "Global World Space" for the creation of globality as a homogeneously imagined world-space through the totalitarian definition of "race" as a structuring

9 In another text she elaborates in regard to Elisabeth Grosz: "Origin stories are always mythic because they posit a beginning of time that is outside of itself, in the sense that it is a monotime that is outside of the flux and continuance of change – outside, as it were, the passage of time" (Yusoff 2015, 21).

 element of difference, and explains: "[T]he tools of nineteenth-century scientific projects of knowledge produced the notion of the racial, which institutes the global as an ontoepistemological context" (Ferreira da Silva 2007, xii–xiii). While the nation-state and rational subject co-produced the modern cosmology internally, "race" as a category draws an outward line of exclusion re-organizing the global space (Ferreira da Silva 2007, 194). In this respect the decolonial theorist Walter Mignolo argues for a similar genesis of globality. In his effort to think of decoloniality as an epistemic practice, he proposes an analysis of colonial epistemology while at the same time delinking from it and opening a space for potential knowledge production. In regard to political theorist Carl Schmitt's concept of global lines and dynamics of land appropriation, Mignolo outlines the imperial notion of globality. Global linear thinking represents a "Western"-modern mode of conceptualizing differences as universal and definite distinctions that striate global space.

> It [1492, as the moment of the bifurcation of history] is the moment, as Carl Schmitt explains, in which 'global linear thinking' is defined and linked to the creation of international law. This moment also created and implemented external and internal colonial differences ... 'Global linear thinking' traced the lines in land and sea *and* racial lines. (Mignolo 2015, 110–11)

In this regard, globality manifests itself in a seemingly universal principle that runs through the colonially defined modern episteme and is brought to light again in the form of "the planetary." What intersects here is the abstract Apollonian gaze and the colonial understanding of nature as a scalable factor of production constituting an "order of things" that poses basic problems of management and control to which cybernetics offers a technocratic answer. Correspondingly, Yusoff emphasizes the conception of a homogenized global entity as the "meta-ontology" of the Anthropocene, that is "not just a political but a material ordering of the world." She notes: "This is why global-world-space is world-making in the sensibility of space rather than simply a descriptive act of spatiality. Global-world-space is the conceit of a global spatiality constructed through uneven geographies of experience and exploitation in order to maintain the privilege of its vision" (Yusoff 2017).

What I have tried to outline with the notion of globality is the asymmetrical relation between the genealogical approaches of cybernetically informed ecology and modernity's colonial foundation, which intersect not least at the Anthropocene. Thereby both suggest historical trajectories as well as possible consequences. But where general ecology is prone to focus on the entangled histories of science, technology and colonialism, the inherently epistemic-political claim of decolonization argues for non-hegemonic potential genealogies that actively unsettle the former.

Partial Perspectives

In the experimental film *4 Waters: Deep Implicancy* (2018) Ferreira da Silva and Arjuna Neuman explore a web of global relations that manifests in the movement of bodies, trajectories of ideas, structures of (neo)colonialism, and ecological devastation mediated and set into action by phase transitions of water. Understanding water not simply as chemical bonds, the film follows it as a medium of passage and transition, an intimate relation between the organic and inorganic. The four waters of the Mediterranean, the Pacific, the Atlantic and the Indian Ocean evoke histories of enforced passages, logistics of goods and ideas that connect via their medium to geological processes and technological infrastructures, Holding space for different forms of navigation—from gut feeling to satellite positioning—water is depicted as indeterminate yet omnipresent matter rendering "all land masses [... as] islands in an ongoing chain of atolls" (Ferreira da Silva and Neuman 2019, 9). As one might swim or dive, ship or drown, the film traces the manifold possibilities of narration, histories and perspectives water bears and thus renders visible genealogies and modes of knowledge production. Portraying an interwoven narration of different layers, *4 Waters* negotiates geological sub-structures and social histories, thereby touching on descriptive statements and cosmologies that are (in-)formed as much by geological processes as by technologies. Liquefaction appears as the effect of a "rumble from beyond measurable time, from before the start of the organic mapping," the narrator's voice states (Ferreira da Silva and Neuman 2018, timecode: 00:15:33). Forgotten layers resurge and corrode the soil for the water to pass up- or downwards. It enforces its various pasts upon the present and proposes a submerged analysis that helps to interpret the magnitude of hypocenters.

[Fig. 2] A tumbling and submerged take following a selfie stick to the ocean's floor. (Still from *4 Waters: Deep Implicancy*, Arjuna Neuman and Denise Ferreira da Silva, 2018, courtesy of the artists)

So contrary to the Apollonian gaze's claim to universality, which Ferreira da Silva and Neuman deliberately integrate visually as well as conceptually, the filmmakers situate it as only one among many forms of knowledge production. With the submerged and partial narrative of the film they suggest that epistemological shifts imply the task of thoroughly working through the unthought and buried, as well as the surfacing, historical conditions. These tend to unfold their effect from a historical distance, yet in denaturalizing and unsettling the solid open spaces for orientation on liquid ground.

The "impure" genealogy of ecology and ecologization here served as an indicator in order to lay out changing modes of thinking and knowledge. It thus exposes how power/knowledge structures and modes of government as well as control are ever related to media-technological evolutions. A "biopolitics of surrounding" (Sprenger 2019) and apparatus of capture aiming at behavior and governing environmental parameters are but two manifestations of ecological modes of subjectivation that are contrasted by "a radically relational and procedural conception of environment" (Hörl 2018, 160). Conceived of as a speculative mode, general ecology suggests a possibility of re-thinking the becoming-environmental not as the sole phenomenon of globality but as a "neocritical project" (Hörl 2017, 5) of an epistemological shift. Albeit this concept touches only partially on what has been argued in regard to Yusoff as reappearing patterns of origin-stories, it manifests as one of various current signatures of the fault line. These patterns then would need to be questioned and shown to be founded on historical constructions and self-referential narratives. Therefore, the political aspect of Wynter's insistence on the importance of a decolonial and processual conception of emergences focuses on the conditions of possible "answers." As Ferreira da Silva suggests: "[I]nstead of the question of who and what we are, we need to go deeper into the investigation of how we come up with answers to the questions" (Ferreira da Silva 2015, 104). What a liquefied order of knowledge thus offers is the possibility of mapping the Anthropocene's fault line in its permanent actualization as a practice of navigation, which asks how epistemic hypocenters are formed in the first place.

References

Clarke, Bruce. 2010. "Information." In *Critical Terms for Media Studies*, edited by W. J. T. Mitchell and Mark B. N. Hansen, 157–71. Chicago: University of Chicago Press.

Clarke, Bruce. 2014. *Neocybernetics and Narrative*. Minneapolis: University of Minnesota Press.

Clarke, Bruce. 2017. "Rethinking Gaia: Stengers, Latour, Margulis." *Theory, Culture & Society* 34 (4): 3–26.

Cosgrove, Denis E. 2001. *Apollo's Eye: A Cartographic Genealogy of the Earth in the Western Imagination*. Baltimore: Johns Hopkins University Press.

Davis, Heather M., and Zoe Todd. 2017. "On the Importance of a Date, or Decolonizing the Anthropocene." *ACME: An International Journal for Critical Geographies* 16 (4): 761–80.

DeLoughrey, Elizabeth M. 2013. "The Myth of Isolates: Ecosystem Ecologies in the Nuclear Pacific." *Cultural Geographies* 20 (2): 167–84.

Ferreira da Silva, Denise. 2007. *Toward a Global Idea of Race*. Minneapolis: University of Minnesota Press.

Ferreira da Silva, Denise. 2015. "Before Man: Sylvia Wynter's Rewriting of the Modern Episteme." In *Sylvia Wynter – On Being Human as Praxis*, edited by Katherine McKittrick, 90–105. Durham, NC: Duke University Press.

Ferreira da Silva, Denise, and Arjuna Neuman. 2018. *4 Waters: Deep Implicancy* [Film].

Ferreira da Silva, Denise, and Arjuna Neuman. 2019. "4 Waters: Deep Implicancy – Correspondence between Denise Ferreira da Silva and Arjuna Neuman." Toronto: Gallery TPW.

Foucault, Michel. 1996. "Nietzsche, Genealogy, History." In *Language, Counter-Memory, Practice – Selected Essays and Interviews*, edited by Donald F. Bouchard, 139–64. Ithaca, NY: Cornell University Press.

Friedrich, Alexander, Petra Löffler, Niklas Schrape, and Florian Sprenger. 2018. *Ökologien der Erde: zur Wissensgeschichte und Aktualität der Gaia-Hypothese*. Lüneburg: meson press.

Golley, Frank B. 1993. *A History of the Ecosystem Concept in Ecology: More than the Sum of the Parts*. New Haven: Yale University Press.

Hartman, Saidyia V., and Frank B. Wilderson. 2003. "The Position of the Unthought." *Qui Parle* 13 (2): 183–201.

Hayles, Katherine. 2017. *Unthought: The Power of the Cognitive Nonconscious*. Chicago: University of Chicago Press.

Hörl, Erich. 2011. "Die technologische Bedingung. Zur Einführung." In *Die technologische Bedingung: Beiträge zur Beschreibung der technischen Welt*, edited by Erich Hörl, 7–53. Berlin: Suhrkamp.

Hörl, Erich. 2017. "Introduction to General Ecology – The Ecologization of Thinking." In *General Ecology: The New Ecological Paradigm*, edited by Erich Hörl and James Burton, 1–73. New York: Bloomsbury Academic.

Hörl, Erich. 2018. "The Environmentalitarian Situation: Reflections on the Becoming-Environmental of Thinking, Power, and Capital." *Cultural Politics* 14 (2): 153–73.

Hui, Yuk. 2017. "On Cosmotechnics: For a Renewed Relation between Technology and Nature in the Anthropocene." *Techné: Research in Philosophy and Technology* 21 (2): 1–23.

Lovelock, James E., and Lynn Margulis. 1974. "Atmospheric Homeostasis by and for the Biosphere: The Gaia Hypothesis." *Tellus* 26 (1–2): 2–10.

Lowenhaupt Tsing, Anna. 2012. "On Nonscalability: The Living World Is Not Amenable to Precision-Nested Scales." *Common Knowledge* 18 (3): 505–24.

Mignolo, Walter D. 2015. "Sylvia Wynter: What Does It Mean to Be Human?" In *Sylvia Wynter: On Being Human as Praxis*, edited by Katherine McKittrick, 106–23. Durham, NC: Duke University Press.

Morton, Timothy. 2009. *Ecology Without Nature: Rethinking Environmental Aesthetics*. Cambridge: Harvard University Press.

Pias, Claus. 2004. "Zeit Der Kybernetik – Eine Einstimmung." In *Cybernetics – Kybernetik. The Macy-Conferences 1946–1953. Band 2. Documents/Dokumente*, edited by Claus Pias, 9–41. Zürich: diaphanes.

Sarasin, Philipp, Silvia Berger, Marianne Hänseler, and Myriam Spörri. 2007. "Bakteriologie und Moderne. Eine Einleitung." In *Bakteriologie und Moderne. Studien zur Biopolitik des Unsichtbaren 1870-1920*, edited by Philipp Sarasin, Silvia Berger, Marianne Hänseler, and Myriam Spörri, 8–43. Frankfurt a.M.: Suhrkamp.

Sprenger, Florian. 2019. *Epistemologien des Umgebens – Zur Geschichte, Ökologie und Biopolitik künstlicher Environments*. Bielefeld: transcript.

Subcommission on Quaternary Stratigraphy. 2019. "Working Group on the 'Anthropocene.'" Accessed May 22, 2020. http://quaternary.stratigraphy.org/working-groups/anthropocene/.

Tiqqun. 2020. *The Cybernetic Hypothesis*. Los Angeles: Semiotext(e).

Waters, Colin N., Jan Zalasiewicz, Colin Summerhayes, Ian J. Fairchild, Neil L. Rose, Neil J. Loader, William Shotyk, et al. 2018. "Global Boundary Stratotype Section and Point (GSSP) for the Anthropocene Series: Where and How to Look for Potential Candidates." *Earth-Science Reviews* 178 (March): 379–429.

Wynter, Sylvia. 2003. "Unsettling the Coloniality of Being/Power/Truth/Freedom: Towards the Human, After Man, Its Overrepresentation – An Argument." *CR: The New Centennial Review* 3 (3): 257–337.

Wynter, Sylvia. 2015. "The Ceremony Found: Towards the Autopoetic Turn/Overturn, Its Autonomy of Human Agency and Extraterritoriality of (Self-)Cognition." In *Black Knowledges/Black Struggles: Essays in Critical Epistemology*, edited by Jason R. Ambroise and Sabine Broeck, 184–252. Liverpool: Liverpool University Press.

Yusoff, Kathryn. 2015. "Anthropogenesis: Origins and Endings in the Anthropocene." *Theory, Culture & Society* 33 (2): 1–26.

Yusoff, Kathryn. 2017. "Epochal Aesthetics: Affectual Infrastructures of the Anthropocene." *E-Flux Architecture – Accumulation*. March 29, 2017. Accessed May 20, 2020. https://www.e-flux.com/architecture/accumulation/121847/epochal-aesthetics-affectual-infrastructures-of-the-anthropocene/.

Yusoff, Kathryn. 2018. *A Billion Black Anthropocenes or None*. Minneapolis: University of Minnesota Press.

Echolocation

Anna Zilahi

We echo each other's words, this way we become reverberations ourselves. We don't know why a new bearing can be born from the constant loss of oneself. We consume what we need, we discharge what we don't. A different chaos nests in our footsteps, but it doesn't empathize. The fog-horn cries out, the fleet of cargo vessels slip their anchors to its sound. Its high price-margin cargo is fixed amidst the swell, the durable material travels towards a slow half-life. The prow cuts through the water, the indifference of solid steel slits the holding ocean into two liquid strands. Our siblings in the water cannot avoid craze, they are moving objects on our radars, we are programme errors on theirs. Their awaited messengers are dissolved in the oil-dense cacophony. We echo each other's words, but we are not each other's points of reference. Deadening solitude. Noise in logic.

Translated by Owen Good

BLUE MARBLE

GOOGLE EARTH

CRITICAL CARTOGRAPHY

GEOBROWSER

INTERACTIVE GLOBE

ENVIRONMENTALISM

[5]

NAVI / GATED / GAZE: Google Earth's Narrative of the Earth and the Privatization of Gaze

Marie Heinrichs

With Google Earth, the pictures "Earthrise" and "Blue Marble"—symbols of the environmental movement and a global community—have come to inhabit our screens as virtual and interactive globes. Free navigational platforms have been considered as democratizing mapping practices. However, little attention has been paid to examining whose perspective it is that these representations are based on, and what this perspective is capable of conveying. In this article, I identify the user interface of Google Earth as a mode of production related to a structure of knowledge and power; inscribed into several forms of maps, this structure implies powerful narratives, which commercial companies can easily capitalize on. Central for Google has been

the narrative of an interconnected global village as an ideology of the future, perfectly visualized in Google Earth: an advertising, user-generated, and editorially created three-dimensional interface that is consumed as representational of a given reality imparts total coverage of the world as progressive, and as supporting environmental claims. Instead, I suggest, the narrative of interconnected globality strengthens the power of Google as a company. Its algorithms guide "our" perception on the world.

Earthrise or the Turning of the Gaze

Towards the end of the 1960s and the beginning of the 1970s, two images became the most reproduced and influential images of the planet: On December 24, 1968, the spacecraft Apollo 8 orbited the Moon, and crewmember William Anders took a picture of the blue Earth at the moment at which it emerged from the shadow of the Moon. The picture, "Earthrise," immortalized on a US stamp, became the symbol of the first Earth Day in 1970. Two years later, in 1972, the crew of Apollo 17 took another picture that finally showed the whole globe, and became known as "Blue Marble." Apollo 17 was the last manned lunar mission. Since then, no humans have been far enough into space to take another picture of the entire globe.

The photographs "Earthrise" and "Blue Marble" decisively influenced our visual frame for and perspective on the world. When thinking about the Earth, we tend think about a distant blue planet. It is a powerful image. As a symbol for the environmental movement, it represented the fragility of "mother Earth." As an abstraction of the global community, it stood for the ideal of an interconnected world. However, when we talk about Earthrise, we talk simultaneously about a turning of the gaze. As artist Anselm Franke puts it: "This turning of the gaze back towards earth signified a change of direction: the expansion-geared, outwards-directed frontier imaginary folding back on itself, in a 180 degrees turn" (2013, 1).

Today, compiled satellite data are embedded in computerized systems of representation and analysis such as geographic information systems (GIS). GIS are, in general, spatial information systems that store, manage, update, analyze and model geo-objects and represent them (alphanumerically and graphically) in a digital system of representation. However, NASA (the US National Aeronautics and Space Administration) still referred to a composite image of the whole globe taken in 2012 by the VIIRS instrument aboard the Earth-observing satellite Suomi NPP as Blue Marble. With geobrowsers—internet-based, virtual and interactive representations of the globe that refer to geodata—such as Google Earth, both pictures inhabit "our" screens, and hence often our homes. Geodata are generated by state and private actors and used ubiquitously. However, little scholarly attention has been paid to examining whose perspective it is that these representations are based on, and what such a perspective is capable of conveying. Can the picture of the whole Earth, represented in computerized maps, authentically reflect environmental claims and values?

By May 2011 more than 1 billion people had downloaded Google Earth (Google Maps (the official blog) 2011). New web-based mappings and free navigational platforms have been considered as "democratizing" change in mapping history (cf. Crampton 2010, 37). Google Earth made GIS technology and data accessible to a large number of people. Geographer Michael Goodchild (cited in Butler 2006, 777) termed it the democratization of GIS, even though the geobrowser is not considered a "true" GIS, since it has limited capabilities. It "implements essentially the same concept, but in a much more restricted sense" (Goodchild 2008, 35).

[Fig. 1] Composite image of the Blue Marble taken from the VIIRS instrument aboard the Earth-observing satellite Suomi NPP (Source: NASA/NOAA/GSFC/Suomi NPP/VIIRS/Norman Kuring 2012)

Access to these technologies is not independent of privileges, however, and these privileges vary worldwide. While access is unevenly spread between countries as well as generations, income, race and education (Crutcher and Zook 2009; Crampton 2003), and the use of mapping services reflects and reinforces racialized cyberspace (Crutcher and Zook 2009), increasingly private actors take advantage of developments in remote sensing systems, data processing and mapping technologies in GIS (Zook and Graham 2007).

My paper seeks to explore the power relations, intrinsic to narratives, underpinning Google Earth. I argue that it is necessary to take into account the inconsistencies and contradictions inherent to perspectives on Earth that are shaped and designed around the symbol of the globe, namely the narrative of an *interconnected global world*. In my research, I will analyze the user interface as akin to production chains or modes of production that are related to structures of knowledge and power. I argue that visualizations of territory reflect this structure, when impulses of centralization and imperialism characterize them. The structure of knowledge and power inscribed into several forms of maps implies powerful narratives and fixed perspectives, which can be used for the gains of commercial companies.

Tools of an Interconnected Global World

The Whole Earth Catalog

Looking at the notions and ideologies that emerged in the wake of the first photographs of the planet helps to understand why these pictures became so powerful in constructing the narrative of an interconnected global world. First, the historical context of these images clarifies their symbolic significance and connection to environmentalism. Second, the narrative of an interconnected global world is strongly tied to the image of the Blue Marble, especially when Google Earth represents it due to its interactive interface.

At the climax of the Cold War, namely the Cuban missile crisis in 1962, the fragility of life on the planet seemed more real than ever before. The possible extinction of humankind and its source of existence, imagined as an anthropomorphic view of the extinction of the whole planet, made Earth's value feasible. The blue globe shines isolated in an immeasurably large universe. In his influential *Operating Manual for Spaceship Earth* (1969), architect Richard Buckminster Fuller imagines a "Spaceship Earth as an integrally-designed machine which to be persistently successful must be comprehended and serviced in total" (16). He continues later: " ... it is highly feasible for all human passengers aboard ... to enjoy the whole ship ..., provided that we are not so foolish as to burn up our ship ..." (40). The Blue Marble, similarly, illustrates technological achievements in manned spaceflight, driven by the Space Race, and Earth's value at the same time.[1] Additionally it represents the beginning of the age of the computer and digital culture, whose developments were imagined as future hope for a united world. Fuller for example imagines: "[W]e are going to resolve the ever-accelerating dangerous impasse of world-opposed politicians and ideological dogma ... by the computer" (42).

A growing number of mainly young people rejected the nuclear arms race and technologies that endangered the integrity of the planet, such as nuclear energy, but felt more optimistic about information technologies that accompanied the invention of the internet (Turner 2006). Many refused ways of living that were regulated by the government, primarily rigid bureaucracies—a rejection that led to various countercultures and political grassroots movements as for example the *New Communalists* in the United States. Scholar in communication Fred Turner developed the term *New Communalists* to distinguish a certain counterculture that promoted information technologies and cybernetic change of the world from others.[2] The New Communalists "embraced small technologies that they hoped would help them live as independent citizens within the kind of universe that [Norbert] Wiener and the Committee [of National Morale] had described, a universe in which all things were interlinked by information" (Turner 2019, 29). Not surprisingly, Steward Brand's *Whole Earth Catalog* provided useful tips for those who dreamed of an interconnected *Global Village* [3] and who sought to create communal ways of living. The catalog listed book or gadget recommendations on topics such as Whole Systems, D-I-Y, Urban

1 The former Soviet Union launched the first satellite *Sputnik 1* on October 4, 1957, which caused the Sputnik crisis in the United States. The fear of a technological gap in the arms race is often given as a reason for the founding of NASA.

2 For a detailed overview of their history up to cyber culture, see Turner 2006.

3 Marshall McLuhan invented the term (McLuhan 1962; 1964). The theories of McLuhan and Richard Buckminster Fuller (e.g., *Ideas and Integrities* 1963) had great influence on the New Communalists.

[Fig. 2] Cover of Steward Brand's Whole Earth Catalog Fall 1968 (Source: https://monoskop.org/images/0/09/Brand_Stewart_Whole_Earth_Catalog_Fall_1968.pdf)

Gardening or Architecture under the slogan *access to tools*. A tool was understood as anything for use. However, the slogan turned technology in general, but more precisely *purchase recommendations, into means of liberation*. In his Stanford University commencement speech, Apple co-founder Steve Jobs had compared the catalog to the search engine Google: "The Whole Earth Catalog ... was one of the bibles of my generation. ... It was sort of like Google in paperback form, 35 years before Google came along. It was idealistic and overflowing with neat tools and great notions" (2005). Almost two million copies of the catalogue were sold. On the cover: the historical photographs of space.

As a symbol for a global ecosphere and world society on the one hand, and individualism and technological progress on the other, the Blue Marble has bridged not only diverse countercultures and environmental movements but also contradictory lifestyles. It is technological progress measured by the individual's purchasing power instead of sustainability. Progress is thus not conceived of as material and relational, that is, interacting with an environment and being tied to its resources. The global connectivity symbolized by the Blue Marble is related to human beings and their individual sphere of action. Prioritizing the mainland, since humankind can (not yet) live under water—although water occupies nearly three quarters of the Earth's surface and makes it appear blue—illustrates one aspect of the inherently anthropocentric nature of this view. New technologies such as smartphones for private users expand the "global" human territory. Designed to satisfy the wants of the individual a smartphone tells nothing about the satellites in space and gold or coltan mines it requires to function (cf. Cohen and Van Balen 2016). In their work artists Revital Cohen and Tuur van Balen have investigated materialities of media technology.[4] In an article about their research trip to the Democratic Republic of the Congo they note:

> The demand for Congolese minerals and organisms has constantly been a direct result of industrial developments, making the Congolese soil the birthplace of objects of desire and destruction that are actualized in other realities, in other parts of the world. The nuclear bombs of Hiroshima and Nagasaki contained parts of the Congo, just as every smartphone and laptop today. (2016, 333)

It is the material realities of media technologies of "modern" everyday life that are not taken into consideration.[5] A digital screen tells nothing about space junk[6] that marks the enlarged

4 In their artwork H/AlCuTaAu, for example, they represent the chemical elements of electronics.

5 For an overview of recent discussions concerning ecological contexts of contemporary media and the Anthropocene, see Parikka 2015 and 2016.

6 "[The] chronological range [of human-made objects in space] is from 1958 (Vanguard 1, the oldest surviving spacecraft) until the present time. In weight, the accumulated debris is estimated to be 6,000 tons" (Gorman 2019, 108).

and "harnessed" territory of man. Fracking technology for instance extends the access below ground level without asking whether more natural gas would be needed if its distribution were thought of in sustainable and communal ways.

By 1984, the New Communalist movement had disappeared, but not their ideas, now realized in offices instead of farms (cf. Turner 2019, 140). Tech groups in the San Francisco Bay area—located close to the offices of the *Whole Earth Catalog* in Menlo Park—had spawned companies that incorporated the ideal of interconnectivity, peer-to-peer information sharing, and individual empowerment. Steward Brand and his networks entrepreneurially linked these groups. Most influential have been, firstly, researchers at Douglas Engelbart's—the inventor of the computer mouse—Augmentation Research Center (ARC) at the Stanford Research Institute (SRI) and later Xerox's Palo Alto Research Center (PARC). Secondly, the Homebrew Computer Club, started by Gordon French and Fred Moore in 1975. Its members complemented each other's ideas on computer technologies (cf. Turner 2019, 106), amongst them being Apple Inc. founders Stephen Wozniak and Steve Jobs.

In 1985, Brand partnered with Larry Brilliant. They used the Whole Earth Catalog as model for a teleconferencing system named the Whole Earth 'Lectronic Link (WELL)—one of the most influential computer networks. Its members mainly came from San Francisco Bay's and Silicon Valley's computer industry. Silicon Valley's economy by then had become the wealthiest in the United States (cf. Turner 2019, 141–174). Companies that incorporated movements that pushed environmental consciousness as well as technological inventions shaped the idea of global community and a technically interconnected world of individuals as a normative ideology for the future. This ideology is explicitly visualized as a virtual interactive globe in the form of Google Earth.

In 1998, the Stanford University students Sergey Brin and Larry Page founded Google Inc.[7] Since 2005, Google has been offering the standard version of the Google Earth software for free. The allowances of the software are threefold. First, it embeds satellite and aerial images into an interface that represents the Earth as a three-dimensional globe. Second, the digital globe creates the illusion of motion, producing a powerful illusion of reality. Third, it allows interaction with other databases, such as coordinates of GPS devices, mapping software, and users.

The interface is composed of different image sources "mosaic'ed together as a patchwork" (Parks 2009, 536). The images were taken at a particular time, by means of a particular image technology, and were distributed by a specific company. A key player today is the private company Digital Globe, which belongs to Maxar Technologies and works closely with Google. It markets images from the GeoEye and World View satellites and IKONOS (decommissioned 2015). The potential for interaction is characterized by the possibility of navigating independently to right, left, top, bottom or "into the earth". Moreover, it is possible to adapt the globe to user demands, for example, by clicking on corresponding boxes in the sidebar or by switching from *Ground View* to *Street View*. As a collaboratively *produced* "networked system of spatial representation" (Farman 2010, 873), it provides access to further data uploaded by other companies or individuals. Google simplifies a collection of databases to a "child-of-ten standard of user interface design" (Goodchild 2008, 34) by avoiding the technical details of geo-referencing.

Google Earth thus made a completely different form of map available. November et al. (2013, 587, transl. by author) even suggest: "Looking at a map today means logging into a navigational platform," characterized by databases, the interface,

7 Restructured to the parent company Alphabet Inc. in 2015.

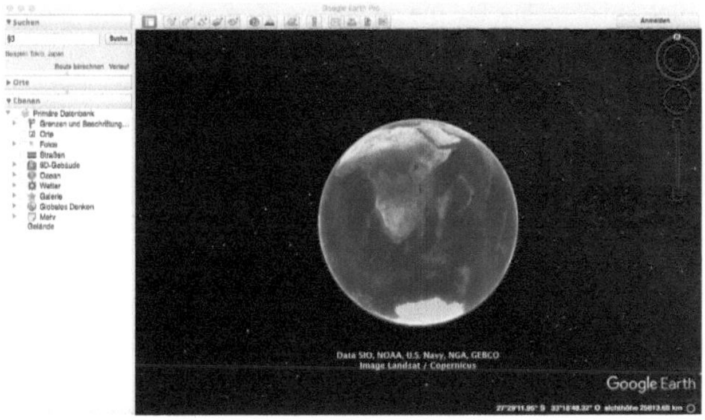

[Fig. 3] Screenshot of the Blue Marble in Google Earth Pro

interconnectivity, and different output options. Even more, it manifests the idea of global participatory geography since expensive satellite imagery became freely accessible. Yet, only every second person worldwide is online, while the percentage of the total population using the internet ranges between 70 and 99 percent mainly in countries of the "Global North" (Maak 2019, 40–41).[8] The Blue Marble has become a digital interactive map and a customizable tool for the routes of "Western" human beings—that is, the colonial construct of "developed, industrialized, urbanized, capitalist, secular, and modern" (Hall 1992, 277) society.

Hidden "Truths" of Three-Dimensional Earth Visualization

In the course of technologization from the 1950s onwards, the representation of maps has changed, but a certain reality of map perception and production has not. As geographer Jeremy Crampton points out, "for critical cartography, mapping is not just

8 There are also differences with regard to internet access in terms of broadband and censorship.

 a reflection of reality, but the *production* of knowledge, and therefore, truth" (2010, 46). Digital mapping technologies are often analyzed and perceived as neutral ("it is just a software!") and factual representations of reality, or as promising technologies for future developments (cf. Crampton 2010, 7–8).[9] But GIS are strongly tied to a history of military practices and to the development of "Western" technologies, and consequently so is Google Earth.[10] Mapping technologies are tied to both methods of cultural interpretation and to modes of production. This includes processes such as modification, governance, and appropriation, which represent specific perspectives imbued with power relations.

Appropriation Processes of Knowledge and Territory

The modes of production of maps can show paradigmatically how, in the course of "Western" history, world networks were "built to mobilise, cumulate and recombine the world" (Latour 1987, 228). Networks that were built up violently and that were built on information enabled, and continue to enable, people to exercise power from a distance. In pointing to networks,

9 The Committee on Beyond Mapping (2006, 47) for example stated: "[GIS] and geographic information science appear to be benign technologies but some of their applications have been questioned; as is true of any technology, GIS, though neutral in and of itself, can be used for pernicious ends."

10 The development of GIS is closely linked to the developments in remote sensing around the first satellites and the internet—both technologies routed in military purposes during the Cold War. However, the potential of geo-information turned out to be useful also for scientific and commercial process analysis on the Earth's surface and in the atmosphere, e.g. for agriculture and forestry, sustainable development, disaster management, and urban planning. Indeed, the first GIS, the Canada Geographic Information System (CGIS), was developed in the 1960s for the Canadian government's then Department of Forestry and Rural Development under the guidance of Roger Tomlinson to store and manipulate the comprehensive data that was collected as part of the Canada Land Inventory (CLI) study (Foresman 1997; Goodchild 2018). Since then, GIS has become a multi-billion dollar industry. For a critical introduction see "Critical GIS" 2005; Crampton 2010, 3.

sociologist of science Bruno Latour enquires about the connections between (universal) knowledge and power so as to question how this knowledge was and is gained and structured (cf. 1987, especially 215–57). By transforming local knowledge through mobile, stable and combinable elements into a new local, however centered, knowledge of the world, an accumulation cycle emerges. The accumulation cycle constitutes an asymmetric knowledge relationship between those who have the centered knowledge of the world and those who have (access to) local knowledge. It is not simply a matter of juxtaposing local and universal knowledge. It is rather a question of "two local knowledges, one of them having the shape of a network" (Latour 1987, 229). The centralizations of knowledge and power are thus inevitably linked and mutually constitutive. Following this, cartography—the study and practice of creating maps—can be described as a network that collects information and fixes perspectives of certain territories. Information from different sources is appropriated, collected, concentrated, combined, structured, and fixed on a medium. As cartographer John Brian Harley claims: "To catalogue the world is to appropriate it … so that all these technical processes represent acts of control over its image, which extend beyond the professed uses of cartography" ([1989] 2011, 287).

Cartography as a network can thus be interpreted as an imperialistic practice. As historian of cartography Matthew Edney argues: "Imperialism and mapmaking intersect in the most basic manner. Both are fundamentally concerned with territory and knowledge" (1997, 1),[11] and consolidate forms of power in accumulation circles. The representation of a chosen area in a certain way creates a political reality framed by the modes of appropriation of knowledge and territory. What does that mean? "Space, in the conventional map, becomes place—the named and the known. Maps are thus imbued with power" (Mitchell 2012, 19).

11 Edney considers how, among other things, the acquisition of knowledge and the creation of spatial representations by actors of the East India Company helped legitimize the colonialist activities of the British Empire.

Maps visualize the integrity of a particular territory. Thus, the map does not only legitimize the empire's territory and existence but inscribes meaning into it (cf. Edney 1997, 2).

In the process of mapping, an area over which knowledge has been gained is represented. It becomes an object of knowledge. This knowledge is based on a *specific* perspective, and bound—in accordance with traditional "Western" epistemology—to the claim of representational objectivity. In her influential examination on "Situated Knowledges" Donna J. Haraway (1991, 183–201) questioned this view. She concluded that knowledge is not a neutral "view from above" but "from somewhere;" it is positioned (Haraway 1991, 196). Accordingly, a specific perspective reflects only one socio-historical position. As feminist standpoint theorists have pointed out, the traditional representational view of knowledge lacks a relational understanding of the world (cf. Harding 2004). However, focusing on its representational character instead of its relational basis has been a powerful tool to deviate knowledge from its material, oppressing effects, and to deviate from it the center of power. Seen this way "[a]ccounts of such objects [of knowledge] can seem to be either appropriations of a fixed and determined world reduced to resource for the instrumentalist projects of destructive Western societies, or they can be seen as masks for interests, usually dominating interests" (Haraway 1991, 197). In contrast to dominated perspectives, dominant ones are ideologically permeated.

Subsequently, a map is never only a visual representation. According to cultural theorist Bernhard Siegert it "is a cultural technique that, in the service of the state, *produced* the territory as a political reality" (2011, 15). Maps create a worldview, i.e., they produce the reality of a certain perspective. The modes of production of a map can therefore be characterized as based on the appropriation of knowledge and territory, including the acquisition and exercise of symbolic power and narrative elements. To create a map means to create powerful narratives. Following Michel Foucault, knowledge and power relations go beyond the localization of power (1980). *Productivity* unfolds through spanning a network:

> Power is employed and exercised through a net-like organisation. And not only do individuals circulate between its threads; they are always in the position of simultaneously undergoing and exercising this power. They are not only its inert or consenting target; they are always also the elements of its articulation. In other words, individuals are the vehicles of power, not its points of application. (Foucault 1980, 98)

The balance of power is by no means only attributed to individual people or groups. To ensure endurance, power forms a productive net that "doesn't only weigh on us as a force that says no, but that ... traverses and produces things, it induces pleasure, forms knowledge, produces discourse" (Foucault 1980, 119). It is not exclusively oppressive. Rather, it cannot be separated from our everyday life and from productivity that can be easily modified for commercial purposes that centralize power. Read in this way, map users fulfill the vehicle function of power. They, although unintentionally or indifferently, maintain and stabilize centralized power networks.

In conclusion, maps create a discourse that inscribes and dictates perspectives of space. This space is not to be experienced but is instead a territory to be conquered—a space that is exposed, vulnerable, and for the viewer to take. Following this, the concept of "globality" affirmed within navigational platforms reflects such a power network. New information and mapping technologies, driven forward by capital and profit, expand the "global" as a source of capital, and therefore influence. New technologies center power and transform ways of life. Nevertheless, they are strengthened, legitimized, and financed by their users. Globality generated by applications therefore is re-narrated as customizable or as technological, economic, and cultural globalization. The next spaces to be explored, appropriated, exploited and visualized—conquered—by companies and state actors, whose technology produces imperial modes of living, will for example be the ocean and outer space. Conquest will be legitimized by technological progress.

The Illusion of Navigational Freedom and Customizable Reality

The dream of cartographic transparency has long been part of Western cartographic genealogy and the "Western" imagination of the Earth. The synoptic *Eye of Apollo* (Cosgrove 2001) finds its visualization in Google Earth's three-dimensional globe. The genealogy reflects the Western imagination of this Earth. Google Earth can thus fulfill and intensify the illusion of global coverage in scaled compartmentalisations of global community, as a territory branded by the company.

As a virtual globe the "digital peep-box" (Kingsbury and Jones 2009) of Google Earth produces the desire for random adventurous movement as well as the perception of panoptical cartographic transparency. The authors contradict Google Earth's solitary Apollonian characteristics and hold the software to be thought of in a Dionysian, that is, an experimental and joyful, manner. Relating to Friedrich Wilhelm Nietzsche's aesthetic theory, Dionysian stands for intoxication that accompanies Apollonian serenity and objectivity (cf. Kingsbury and Jones 2009, 504). Other scholars point to the counter-cultural, artistic, and activist potential of free navigational platforms, including Google Earth. It engages its users to participate in cartographic debate due to its accessibility and interactive potential (Farman 2010, 870). Indeed, open-source aerial imagery has been used as a critique tool, exemplified by the extractive geopolitics project "Imaginando Buenas" that searches for globally dispersed alterations of the Earth via Google Earth (kollektiv orangotango+ 2018, 240–43). Anthropologist Stefan Helmreich (2011, 1231f.) also points to the potential of creating counter-maps that demonstrate climate change or illustrate environmental concerns, mentioning the visualization of the Pacific trash vortex. However, its representational use reinforces an inherent rhetoric of truth.

Concerning private use, even at short distances, the agency of navigation is quickly left to the system. It is the system that zooms, scrolls, and rotates the navigational modes, while the human actor is only able to perform these tasks separately (cf. Abend and Thielmann 2011, 135). In addition, people rarely rely on their own geographical knowledge and instead seek to consult and rely on Google's accuracy and the accuracy of data. The navigational freedom in Google Earth that resembles the locomotion character of a computer game, in conjunction with the aspiration of universal cartographic capture, rather, as geographer Vera della Dora suggests, intensifies a powerful illusion of reality; a new "rhetoric of truth" (Della Dora 2012, 7) open to the user's demands. The "connection of maps and GIS to 'reality' is typically an inherent expectation of map users and is implemented through something as simple as charting your route to work ..." (Farman 2010, 874)—an assumption we reaffirm as soon as we search for hotel addresses or navigate through a foreign city with Google Maps or Street View. This assumption is also generally reflected in a scientific approach in which the results are seen as representative and objective. Satellite images and aerial photographs serve to manifest this expectation, as the precision of depicted detail is confused with objective reality. These expectations and assumptions are thus felt and perceived, even when the mosaic-like nature of data and images constitute the user interface, and even when the conceptualized space is the result of editing and governance processes, which illustrate only certain details and "suppress ... truth to help the user see what needs to be seen" (Monmonier 1996, 25).

The user is left to *consume* an advertising, user-generated and editorially created interface—that creates the narrative of an easily accessible "panopticon"—*as representational of a given reality***.** The user experiences an abstraction of Earth "as a medium of the past [rather] than of the present" (Parks 2009,

540), *guided* by the platform's algorithms and therefore prone not to question what is not visible. As scholar in science and technology Sheila Jasanoff examines: "Features that loom large on Earth vanish when seen from space" (Jasanoff 2004, 40)—or seen from Google Earth. Concrete conditions and experiences either disappear or are absent from this manageable world: the working hours in cobalt mines, the droughts, the monsoons, the extinction of species, the hunger, the people without homes and without internet access. The realities of experiences on Earth in the "Anthropocene" disappear as well as the realities of Earth's materials that technical devices are based on (cf. Parikka 2016). In light of increasing global warming and social inequality, *relational* counter-maps are absolutely indispensable. Here, the publication *This Is Not an Atlas* (kollektiv orangotango+ 2018) collects numerous ways of creating counter-cartographies that create visibility of "minor" concerns.

However, the Blue Marble remains as the perspective of a privileged "Global North", which does not seem to be, or at least does not perceive itself, as dependent on local conditions (cf. Jasanoff 2004). These invisible realities of the image of the Blue Marble, I suggest, remain invisible even with counter-cultural and counter-hegemonic appropriations of Google Earth. Instead, the narrative of global environmentalism is reproduced and continued as environmentalism linked to global coverage, made possible by Google's software. Thus, the company gets a tool to portray itself as an environmental campaigner. Scholar in science and technology Yaakov Garb's 1985 article on *the use and misuse of the Whole Earth image* could be updated with the addition of Google's interactive map.

Google's Interconnected Territory

Let me recall: the modes of production characterize editing and appropriation processes linked to geo-information and its governance. As one form or visualization of cartographic praxis, navigational platforms demonstrate that whenever data are collected, centralized, and combined, these acts constitute a form of symbolic power that is able to create a power relation that has material effects, stabilized by means of power transmitters. I identified modes of production as part of Google Earth's user interface—and even further as an inherent truth of Western presentations of "the world." As with any map, Google Earth is a projection of the world based on a specific perspective, and a projection of totality. As such, it has the potential to shape geographical imaginations. This essential reality of a map's formation history and process, inscribed into its various forms, is not only afforded insufficient attention by consumers—it is the taken-for-granted reality in scientific use of these maps, by nature of our perception of GIS as objective representations of a given reality.

Finally, I argue that Google understands and claims this symbolic power as the operator of the software. "By representing the new global village as a virtual globe that can be navigated and interacted with, Google has taken the steps to chart out visually the territory that it has sought to command: an interconnected global village" (Farman 2010, 877). The claim to, or at least aspiration for, symbolic power lies precisely in the creation of narrative elements and in the creation of elements that influence our everyday lives and which ensure the preservation of this power. The future ideology of a global, digitally networked "village" is a central element of Google's narrative. It is substantiated by a consistent rhetoric of customization and the democratic potential of the Web 2.0 (Crutcher and Zook 2009) and has already been unmasked as, for example, "surveillance capitalism" (Zuboff 2019) or "networks without cause" (Lovink 2011).

However, Google still advertises the narrative of interconnected globality. It demonstrates its ongoing success. Additionally, Google is branding itself as an environmental campaigner: "Our tools are built to help everyone reduce their environmental impact, understand the planet, and take sustainable action.

 By mapping the world's forests and fisheries, our technology is making it easier for policymakers, researchers, and nonprofits to monitor the pulse of the planet" (Google Environmental Report 2019, 7). These exact narratives orbit also, as I have already argued, the first images of the Blue Marble. Whatever the potential of using Google Earth may be, global coverage won't solve the problem of anthropogenic global warming.

Rather, the narratives of interconnected, customizable globality and coverage make us dependent on private communication and navigation technologies, for example, instant messengers, search engines, email programs, route planners, or social media. Digital services seem to have become necessary for survival in a digitalized society. Consequently, they have become fundamental societal infrastructures (of telecommunication) built by private companies, including official communication tools, car-sharing products complementing public transportation systems, or banking processes connected to smartphones. The narratives produce dependency on the internet, a space in which we constantly leave traces—including CO2 footprints—and reveal data that can then be used for targeted practices such as online advertising. These traces thus produce potential capital. The reality the user decodes or produces, such as uploaded photographs of points of interest, are bound to the Policy Terms of Google,[12] which means to their targeting practices. Amnesty International has criticized Google's "surveillance based-business" as a "threat to human rights" (Amnesty International 2019).

12 "We collect information about your activity in our services ... The activity information we collect may include terms you search for, videos you watch, views and interactions with content and ads, voice and audio information when you use audio features, purchase activity, people with whom you communicate or share content, activity on third-party sites and apps that use our services and Chrome browsing history." (Google Policy Terms 2020)

There have already been a number of cases against Google for breaking EU competition law and for its "abuse of a dominant position in the online advertising market," in 2017, 2018, and 2019 (cf. Mrohs 2019). However, the high fines have little effect on its market dominance. Rather, due to their growing reach and economic position, large technological corporations such as Google or Facebook expand their spheres of influence. In the political sphere for instance, state actors are dependent on technology from private companies. Moreover, targeted advertising influences voting behavior, which in turn shapes the political sphere, exemplified strikingly by the Cambridge Analytica scandal in 2018. Further, the narrative of digital "globality" serves to withdraw them from the (legal) responsibility of local jurisdictions. And when a law does take effect, it changes little in the way of Google's market position.

This means that whenever privatized software is used and embedded in "our" everyday lives, power is centralized and transferred, and capital accumulated. The power of map production has shifted from state actors to private companies and their programmers and administrators. While the software is provided free of charge and therefore open to all, "its goal is about (re) constructing a political economy of cartographic information that will drive profits into the coffers of a new class of mapmakers" (Dodge 2013). Google controls its commercially driven codes of representations and decides what information is included and excluded (Zook and Graham 2007).[13] The state imperialism of the past is ensued by private imperialism. Google's territory presents itself in Google Earth as a networked, global village purporting to care for environmentalism and democratizing developments. By creating these narratives in the form of a network it keeps itself and its financial capital not only alive—it expands it. Maps should always be examined primarily as a political practice within which

13 Besides state-led censorship and private concerns on detailed images.

 economic capital is accumulated—and this is true for analogue and virtual maps alike.

In summary, each use of privatized software that is deeply embedded in "our" everyday lives enforces power. Thus, companies like Google increasingly influence their user's perception of the world. It becomes a gated (world) view that enforces colonial representational epistemology and capitalism. It becomes—as I will call it—a *NAVI/GATED/GAZE*.[14] The *view from outside* is one that transmits power. The privatization of gaze has an effect on our behavior. The journey to distant countries is designed as a "destination shopping" of each individual pixel. The Earth's resources are sold with the target vectors of the virtual globe as "world experience" and "exchange." The panoptical view of the user interface makes us believe that we have captured Earth, making it, in its entirety, at our disposal. As former Google senior technologist Michael Jones (2013) argues:

> It's not the map itself that has changed. You would recognize a 1940 map and the latest, modern Google map as having almost the same look. But the old map was a fixed piece of paper, the same for everybody who looked at it. The *new map is different for everyone* who uses it. You can drag it *where you want to go*, you can zoom in *as you wish*, you can switch modes—traffic, satellite—you can fly across your town, even ask questions about restaurants and directions. So, a map has gone from a static, stylized portrait of the Earth to a dynamic, interactive conversation *about your use of the Earth* [emphasis added by author].

As valuable as the comparison of satellite images can be for the scientific community in order to detect and draw attention to changes such as global warming, we have to acknowledge that the turn of our gaze to Earth has simultaneously detached us

14 A circumstance that Siva Vaidhyanathan even terms *The Googlization of Everything* (2012).

from it. In creating an interactive, customizable, and therefore ludically charged global village and "shopping destination," we have also consumed Earth—by "googling" products, expecting global food in supermarkets or taking airplanes for weekend trips—resulting in anthropogenic climate change. Each use of the software, additionally, reproduces Google's narrative of participating in the aim of raising awareness of global warming. In reality, Google is only interested in the profitability of its tools.

Is it surprising that the turning of gaze became a privatization of gaze, thinking about the direction the first images from space moved towards? The photographs from space orbit in the *Whole Earth Catalog* and those utilized by other environmentalist movements were engrossed by the stories of companies like Google or Apple.[15] They stay an abstraction, visualize an "above all things" attitude, and are cultivated in the platforms and gadgets of companies as seemingly suggested solutions. The Earth as the basis of and for life has been turned into a play ball, into an *experience platform globe* that does not involve responsibility, other than its consumption. The viewpoints of the platforms of industrial big capital merely represent "*the power to see/know and not act*" (Parks 2009, 540). It will always be about our *use of* the world. Whatever the potential of the commercially owned images and maps of our planet is, its representations and commercial utilization do not call for any action other than to consume it.

The Blue Marble has been turned into a symbol by private companies that claim to be progressive environmentalists. "We" do not *see* with Google Earth and we are not called into responsibility when playing with the virtual globe. We are nowhere but at our desk, while yearning for an outside world to consume. We might be already booking our next flight. If environmental movements seek to make use of "their" symbol the Blue Marble, it has to be understood and examined within the context

15 Just think of the Apple Earth Day commercial in 2019: "Shot on iPhone XS – Don't mess with Mother."

 of its origin as well as its privatized re- and de-contextualization. As such, the globe is no longer a symbol of "nature" and no longer stands for the fragility of "mother Earth." It might serve, however, as a pressing visualization of the inherent link between capitalism and the human-made, state-led, potentially irreversible damages to the planet. If so, it should be a symbol that reminds those who seek to create and consume the interconnected global village of the costs of the journey.

Thanks to my twin sister, who is never tired of structuring my chaotic thoughts.

References

Abend, Pablo, and Tristan Thielmann. 2011. "Die Erde als Interface. Ein Google Earth-Rundgang." In *Raum als Interface*, edited by Annika Richterich and Gabriele Schabacher, 127–43. Siegen: universi.

Amnesty International. 2019. *Surveillance Giants: How the Business Model of Google and Facebook Threatens Human Rights*. Accessed June 2, 2020. https://www.amnesty.org/download/Documents/POL3014042019ENGLISH.PDF.

Apple. 2019. "Shot on iPhone XS – Don't mess with Mother – Apple." *YouTube*, April 17. Accessed March 30, 2020. https://www.youtube.com/watch?v=Fmhdx_kRd-w.

Butler, Declan. 2006. "The web-wide world." *Nature* 439: 776–78.

Cohen, Revital, and Tuur Van Balen. 2016. "Take a Good Lamp." *Cultural Politics* 12 (3): 332–38.

Committee on Beyond Mapping. 2006. *Beyond Mapping: Meeting National Needs through Enhanced Geographic Information Science*. Washington, DC: The National Academies Press.

Cosgrove, Denis. 2001. *Apollo's Eye: A Cartographic Genealogy of the Earth in the Western Imagination*. Baltimore: Johns Hopkins University Press.

Crampton, Jeremy. 2003. *The Political Mapping of Cyberspace*. Edinburgh: Edinburgh University Press.

Crampton, Jeremy. 2010. Mapping: *A Critical Introduction to Cartography and GIS*. Malden, MA: Wiley-Blackwell.

"Critical GIS". 2005. *Carthographica* 40 (4).

Crutcher, Michael, and Matthew Zook. 2009. "Placemarks and Waterlines: Racialized Cyberspaces in Post-Katrina Google Earth." *Geoforum* 40: 523–34.

Della Dora, Veronica. 2012. "A World of 'Slippy Maps': Google Earth, Global Visions, and Topographies of Memory." *Transatlantica Online* 2: 1–21. Accessed March 22, 2020. http://journals.openedition.org/transatlantica/6156.

Dodge, Martin. 2013. "Review of A Hitory Of The World In Twelve Maps by Jerry Brotton." *Societyandspace.org*, March 25. Accessed March 23, 2020. https://www.societyandspace.org/articles/a-history-of-the-world-in-twelve-maps-by-jerry-brotton.

Edney, Matthew H. 1997. *Mapping an Empire: The Geographical Construction of British India 1765–1843*. Chicago: University of Chicago Press.

Farman, Jason. 2010. "Mapping the digital Empire. Google Earth and the process of postmodern cartography." *New Media & Society* 12 (6): 869–88.

Franke, Anselm. 2013. In "The Whole Earth: In Conversation with Diedrich Diederichsen and Anselm Franke. Interviewer: Ana Teixeira." *eflux Journal* 45. Accessed March 27, 2019. https://www.e-flux.com/journal/45/60114/the-whole-earth-in-conversation-with-diedrich-diederichsen-and-anselm-franke/.

Foresman, Timothy W., ed. 1997. *The History of Geographic Information Systems: Perspectives from the Pioneers*. Upper Saddle River, NJ: Prentice-Hall.

Foucault, Michel. 1980. *Power/Knowledge: Selected Interviews and Other Writings 1972–1977*, edited by Colin Gordon. New York: Pantheon Books.

Fuller, R. Buckminster. 1963. *Ideas and Integrities: A Spontaneous Autobiographical Disclosure*. Englewood Cliffs, NJ: Prentice-Hall.

Fuller, R. Buckminster. 1969. *Operating Manual for Spaceship Earth*. Carbondale: Southern Illinois University Press. http://designsciencelab.com/resources/OperatingManual_BF.pdf.

Garb, Yaakov. 1985. "The Use and Misuse of the Whole Earth image." *Whole Earth Review* 45: 18–25.

Goodchild, Michael F. 2008. "The use cases of digital earth." *International Journal of Digital Earth* 1: 31–42.

Goodchild, Michael F. 2018. "Reimagining the history of GIS." *Annals of GIS* 24 (1): 1–8. https://doi.org/10.1080/19475683.2018.1424737.

Google Environmental Report. 2019. Accessed March 31, 2020. https://services.google.com/fh/files/misc/google_2019-environmental-report.pdf.

Google Maps (the official blog). 2011. "Google Earth downloaded more than one billion times." October 5. Accessed December 10, 2020. https://maps.googleblog.com/2011/10/google-earth-downloaded-more-than-one.html.

Google Policy Terms. 2020. Effective March 31. Accessed April 7, 2020. https://policies.google.com/privacy?hl=en-US.

Gorman, Alice. 2019. "Ghosts in the Machine. Space Junk and the Future of Earth Orbit." *Architectural Design* 89 (1): 106–11.

Hall, Stuart. 1992. "The West and the Rest: Discourse and Power." In *Formations of Modernity: Understanding Modern Societies: An Introduction*, edited by id. and Bram Gieben, 275–320, Cambridge: Polity Press.

Haraway, Donna J. 1991. *Simians, Cyborgs, and Women: The Reinvention of Nature*. New York: Routledge.

Harding, Sandra. 2004. "Introduction. Standpoint Theory as a Site of Political, Philosophic, and Scientific Debate." In *The Feminist Standpoint Theory Reader: Intellectual and Political Controversies*, edited by id., 1–15, New York/London: Routledge.

Harley, John Brian. (1989) 2011. "Deconstructing the Map." In *Classics in Cartography: Reflections on Influential Articles from Cartographica*, edited by Martin Dodge, 273–94. Chichester: John Wiley & Sons.

Helmreich, Stefan. 2011. "From Spaceship Earth to Google Ocean: planetary Icons, Indexes, and Infrastructures." *Social Research* 78 (4): 1211–42.

Jasanoff, Sheila. 2004. "Heaven and Earth." In *Earthly Politics: Local and Global in Environmental Governance*, edited by id. and Marybeth Long Martello, 31–52, Cambridge/London: MIT Press.

Jobs, Steve. 2005. "Stanford Commencement Address, June 12." *Stanford News*, June 14. Accessed March 26, 2020. https://news.stanford.edu/2005/06/14/jobs-061505/.

Jones, Michael. 2013. In James Fallows (Interviewer). "Google's Michael Jones on How Maps Became Personal." *The Atlantic*, January 3. Accessed March 30, 2020. https://www.theatlantic.com/technology/archive/2013/01/googles-michael-jones-on-how-maps-became-personal/266781/.

Kingsbury, Paul, and John Paul Jones III. 2009. "Walter Benjamin's Dionysian Adventures on Google Earth." *Geoforum* 40: 502–13.

kollektiv orangotango+, ed. 2018. *This Is Not an Atlas: A Global Collection of Counter-Cartographies*. Bielefeld: transcript.

Latour, Bruno. 1987. *Science In Action: How To Follow Scientists And Engineers Through Society.* Cambridge: Harvard University Press.

Lovink, Geert. 2011. *Networks Without a Cause: A Critique of Social Media*. Cambridge: Polity Press.

Maak, Niklas. 2019. "Klimakiller Internet." In *Atlas der Globalisierung. Welt in Bewegung*, 40-41. Berlin: Le Monde diplomatique.

McLuhan, Marshall. 1962. *The Gutenberg Galaxy: The Making of Typographic Man*. London: Routledge & Kegan Paul.

McLuhan, Marshall. 1964. *Understanding Media: The Extensions of Men*. New York: McGraw-Hill.

Mitchell, Peta. 2012. *Cartographic Strategies of Postmodernity: The Figure of the Map in Cotemporary Theory and Fiction*, New York: Routledge.

Monmonier, Mark. 1996. *How to Lie with Maps*. Chicago: University of Chicago Press.

Mrohs, Lorenz. 2019. "Online-Werbung: EU-Kommission verhängt Milliardenstrafe gegen Google." *Netzpolitik.org*, March 21. Accessed March 28, 2019. https://netzpolitik.org/2019/online-werbung-eu-kommission-verhaengt-milliardenstrafe-gegen-google/.

November, Valérie, Eduardo Camacho-Hübner, and Bruno Latour. 2013. "Das Territorium ist die Karte. Raum im Zeitalter digitaler Navigation." In *Akteur-Medien-Theorie*, edited by Tristan Thielmann and Erhard Schüttelpelz, 583–614. Bielefeld: transcript.

Parks, Lisa. 2009. "Digging into Google Earth: An Analysis of 'Crisis in Darfur'." *Geoforum* 40: 535–45.

Parikka, Jussi. 2015. *Geology of Media*. Minneapolis/London: University of Minnesota Press.

Parikka, Jussi. 2016. "Deep Times of Planetary Trouble." *Cultural Politics* 12 (3): 279–92.

Siegert, Bernhard. 2011. "The map is the territory." *Radical Philosophy* 169: 13–16. Accessed June 2, 2020. https://www.radicalphilosophyarchive.com/issue-files/rp169_article3_mapistheterritory_siegert.pdf.

Turner, Fred. 2006. *From Counterculture to Cyberculture: Stewart Brand, the Whole Earth Network, and the Rise of Digital Utopianism*. Chicago/London: The University of Chicago Press.

Turner, Fred. 2019. "Machine Politics: The Rise of the Internet and a New Age of Authoritarianism." *Harper's Magazine* 1: 25–33. Accessed March 22, 2020. https://fredturner.stanford.edu/wp-content/uploads/Turner-Machine-Politics-Harpers-Magazine-2019-01.pdf.

Vaidhyanathan, Siva. 2012. *The Googlization of Everything (And Why We Should Worry)*. Berkeley: University of California Press.

Zook, Matthew A., and Mark Graham. 2007. "The creative reconstruction of the Internet: Google and the privatization of cyberspace and DigiPlace." *Geoforum* 38: 1322–43.

Zuboff, Shoshana. 2019. *The Age of Surveillance Capitalism: The Fight for a Human Future at the New Frontier of Power*. New York: Public Affairs.

Ant-Colonial Consciousness & Planetary Consciousness

Kornélia Deres

According to the latest research, a single ant colony rules half the world, their European settlement stretches six thousand kilometres along the coast of the Mediterranean Sea. Members of the megacolony tolerate one another even if they come from several thousand kilometres apart, while unfamiliar ants are received with aggression. Upon meeting, ants gathered from separate continents behave as though they'd always known one another: as friends, as family. As though they shared a common consciousness. According to some, when the planet reaches boiling point, the commandant will appear in the image of an angel. By which time it's certain: our treasure preserved by consciousness and language has been lost.

Translated by Owen Good

BIOSPHERE

ECOSYSTEM

SPACE COLONIALISM

SYMBIOSIS

ENVIRONMENT

[6]

A Laboratory for Living Off-World: Re-Narrating *Biosphere 2*

Hannah Schmedes

With the aid of the story of Biosphere 2 that marked the creation of the world's first large-scale closed ecosystem laboratory, this paper connects extra-terrestrial colonialism to ecology and ecosystem science. The major narrative of the Biosphere 2 project follows closed systems theory and the possibility of human life on Mars. It also states that the experiment failed. In what follows, this narrative is contextualized and searched for its blind spots. The development of the project, its underlying epistemic assumptions and its paradigmatic figureheads are tracked and surveyed. Secondly, another possible narrative is outlined with the perspective of ants and cockroaches, highlighting symbiosis and co-dependence.

I broke my rib in California.
Lynn Margulis

The endosphere turned out to be an exo-sphere. The only environment to live in turned out to be outside.
Sabine Höhler

In 1991, *Biosphere 2* was built in the desert near Oracle, Arizona. Designed as a closed ecosystem that only received two elements from the outside world—sunlight and energy—the monumental glass house served as a temporary home for more than 4,000 species of plants and animals, as well as eight human scientists. Inside, different habitats were simulated: *Biosphere 2* hosted an ocean including a coral reef, a tropical rain forest and mangrove swamp, a desert, agricultural plots, and living and research areas for the human inhabitants. All these habitats, distributed on 1.6 hectares of artificial land, were supposed to simulate and serve as a copy of the first biosphere—the Earth. The first mission, namely the first experiment in *Biosphere 2*, lasted for two years.[1] From 1991 to 1993, all the inhabitants led a life almost completely independent from the outside world. Within the two years, it was to be tested *if* and *how* a completely self-sufficient life under the closed glass dome would work and how the ecosystem would evolve. Two years is about the time it takes for a crewed spacecraft to travel to Mars. In fact, the glass dome was built on behalf of the *Space Biosphere Ventures*, in order to prove if it

1 In 1994, another similar experiment began. It should have run for 10 months, but was ended after six months because two former biospherians broke into the sealed environment. They opened several air-locks and broke glass windows in order to warn the inhabitants because "they believed [Steve] Bannon was going to cut funds that maintained the environmental systems" (Niller 2016). Bannon was hired by Space Biosphere Ventures to manage the finances and reduce cost overruns (Reider 2009, 205–10).

[Fig. 1] An overview of the biospheric architecture: (1) rainforest; (2) savannah/ocean/marsh; (3) desert; (4) intensive agriculture; (5) habitat; (7) south lung; (8) energy center; (9) cooling towers (Source: Dempster 1999, 34)

could serve as a materially independent ecosystem and model for extraterrestrial colonial homes for astronauts. Besides, it was a great way to test the internal Earth atmosphere for its stability. Accordingly, it also acted as a glimpse of future developments on Earth, almost as a glass globe in which predictions of climate change could manifest (Nelson 2019, vii–xii). Starting from the beginning, the enclosure experiment was constantly accompanied by the narrative of its failure. Tracing this narrative, the underlying anthropocentric focus becomes evident. In order to challenge this exclusively human alignment, I will seek to resituate the story of *Biosphere 2* without ignoring its entanglement in space exploration research, ecosystem science, and colonialism.

Sky-Floating Geodesic Spheres

Biosphere 2 served as a medium of prediction, designed as a rigorously constructed laboratory: "Precisely because in the case of ecosystems predicting the future is only possible in the form of probabilities, this model of the Earth should generate future knowledge under controlled experimental conditions" (Bühler 2012, 187; my translation). These controlled conditions were ensured by the integrity of the ecosystem. The glass shell served as a partition to separate the internal environment from the exterior. The concept and structure of the glass dome were designed by Peter Jon Pearce, a former student of the architect Richard Buckminster Fuller (Zabel 1996). Fuller's concept of "geodesic domes" was in turn the inspiration for the architecture of *Biosphere 2*. The first Fuller dome with the name "Biosphère" was exhibited at the 1967 Expo in Montréal as a pavilion of the United States. Two years later, Fuller published his seminal book *Operating Manual for Spaceship Earth*, which postulated that cabin-ecology engineering could solve environmental problems on Earth ([1969] 2017, 57–60). In his 1968 interview with *PLAYBOY*, Fuller even envisions future mobile homes as "sky-floating geodesic spheres" that could encapsulate cities as big as mid-Manhattan in order to stop the "depletion of our planet's productive surface" (1968, 230). His vision is deeply connected with the idea of "free Man." Fuller contends that "[q]uite clearly, man free to enjoy all of his planet, free to research the bottom of his ocean and to re-explore earlier patterns of man's life on earth, will also be swiftly outward-bound to occupy ever greater ranges of the universe." (1968, 230) In the same interview, he also gives a quite basic idea of what cabin-ecology design is:

> When astronauts go beyond the vacuum-bottle-and-sandwich excursion limits, all the regenerative conditions provided naturally by the great biological interactions within the biosphere around the earth's surface will have to be reproduced—in a miniaturized and capsuled human ecology. (Fuller 1968, 228)

The term "cabin ecology" was coined by scholars in astronautics in the late 1950s to describe the requirements needed to recreate an Earth-like environment in a spaceship. In his paper *The Ecological Colonization of* Space, historian Peder Anker found that "cabin-ecology research was sponsored by the military, which considered this topic to be vital to the construction of submarines, atomic shelters, and environmental planning" (2005, 240). Biologist Eugene Pleasants Odum, whose book *Fundamentals of Ecology* popularized the concept of ecosystems, was one of the first participants at the *Human Ecology in Spaceflight Conferences* at Princeton. At the first conference, held in 1963, he elaborated a solution to the problem on how to engineer a cabin ecology suitable for human life. One could create a "stable, self-supporting, moderately complex system by first adding a large number of components to a closed vessel and then allowing the system itself to select those components that will function under a given light-temperature regime" (Calloway 1966, 85). At the core of Odum's ecosystem concept lies the assumption that the biosphere contains distinct, functional units, which are determined by the interactions of contained organisms and the inanimate environment (Odum and Barrett [1953] 1971, 4–6). As simple as it sounds, the glass dome of *Biosphere 2* was grounded on the concept of cabin ecology, and its design considered the inside habitats as distinct units that could be maintained by building a glass wall around them.

The Fuller Dome also inspired hippie and new age communities to use it as a design for buildings in alternative communities. The underlying concept of geodesic domes was fitting, since their ecological implications could be metaphorically transferred to communal life: the solid structure of the domes is ensured by the interaction of individual struts, which *together* form a strong and resilient framework. The ecovillage Synergia Ranch, founded by the Institute for Ecotechnics in 1969, had a similar self-understanding. The ecological field project served to restore a 130-acre landscape in the Santa Fe area of New Mexico that was desertified due to overgrazing. The institute's so-called eco-engineering and synergetic approach was to consider the individual as part of a system in which everything is fully interconnected. The purpose of the Synergia Ranch was partly to develop "a new discipline; interrelating ecosystems, including man, his cultures, and his technosphere with the evolving biospheric totality on the planet earth" (Allen, Nelson, and Parrish 1984, 205). The inhabitants of the Ranch aimed to create three balanced workspaces: ecology, enterprise, and theater. The Theater of All Possibilities, a world-traveling acting group founded by systems ecologist John P. Allen, had been based at the Synergia Ranch and was transferred to *Biosphere 2* (Reider 2009, 23–42 & 131; Nelson 2018a, 16 & 196). Allen was also founder of the Institute of Ecotechnics and created the Space Biosphere Ventures Group, as well as the idea for *Biosphere 2*, for which he served as executive chairman (Broad 1986; Nelson 2018a, 12). He was fascinated by Fuller's concept of synergy, and even invited him to the Galactic Conference in 1982, in yet another location of the Institute of Ecotechnics in Les Marronniers, France (Institute of Ecotechnics 1982).

[Fig. 2] Buckminster Fuller speaking at the Galactic Conference in 1982 (Source: Mignano 2015)

Every biospherian of the first mission was a member of the Institute of Ecotechnics or Synergia Ranch (Reider 2009, 136f.). The $250 million project of *Biosphere 2* was funded by the entrepreneur and oil heir Edward Bass, who participated at theater workshops at Synergia Ranch. Bass was intrigued by Allen's ecological philosophy and eventually became the director of the Institute for Ecotechnics. His intention was to gain profit from the *Biosphere 2* project, turning it into an "ecological Disneyland" (Broad 1991; Anker 2005, 256).[2] Like Allen, Bass believed that space technology would play a crucial role in solving future environmental and social problems on Earth. In a short article on environmental responsibility from 2000, Allen reports that the conference initiating *Biosphere 2* hosted the astronaut Rusty Schweikart, who conveyed the tender feeling of seeing planet Earth from space. Allen encourages Schweikart's depiction by saying that "humankind had changed the face of the planet and had to acknowledge responsibility" (2000, 264), which could be regarded as a description of the basal Anthropocene thesis—which conceptualizes the human as geological force—*avant la lettre*. He also gives credit to activist and author Stewart Brand for pressuring NASA (US National Aeronautics and Space Administration) to release its now-renowned *Earthrise* photographs, which astronaut William Anders had taken during the Apollo 8 flight in 1968 and that adorn Brand's *Whole Earth Catalog*. Allen claims, "[s]eeing the planet as a whole supported the idea of thinking of it as a total system and solving the problems at hand on the right scale" (2000, 264).

By conceptualizing *Biosphere 2* as a miniaturized and capsuled *Biosphere 1*, the cabin ecology was said to be a decal of "natural habitats," whereas there was no resemblance to a "natural" environment that was imitated, but rather a simulation of nature resulting from a selection process conducted by biologists, ecologists, technicians, and engineers. Contextualizing the formation process of *Biosphere 2* shows that the experiment was less about adapting space habitats to nature—that is, according to local ecological conditions and relations—than it was to adapt nature, or more precisely a local earthly habitat, to the needs of space exploration research.

2 When the *Biosphere 2* project was conceptualized, Florida's *Walt Disney World* opened a new attraction called Spaceship Earth in 1982, resembling Fuller's geodesic dome design.

Outlaws

The *Earthrise* photographs represented a visual axis from the outside that philosopher and sociologist Bruno Latour has referred to as the "the view from nowhere" or "the vantage point of Sirius" (2018, 68 & 77). This sight of planet Earth from space is considered a world historical event and credited with introducing a major shift in consciousness regarding new holistic conceptions of the "Earth as system" (Franke 2013, 13). From this extraterrestrial vantage point, the Earth appears like a blue planet among other planets "as a giant space cabin sailing through space with human astronauts onboard" (Anker 2005, 244). The image has not only fueled ecological debates but also contributed to a "unique alliance ... between psychedelia and computer culture, between hippies, proponents of cybernetics, back-to-nature romantics, and technology worshippers who shared a common rejection of hierarchical power structures and authoritarian institutions and went in search for utopian *outlaw areas*" (Franke 2013, 14f.). In 1970, Brand published a supplement to his *Whole Earth Catalog*, titled *The Outlaw Area*, in which "he identified a central nexus of ecological catastrophe and population explosion" (Scott 2016, 9), declaring it inevitable that humanity would reach out to outlaw areas, such as outer space (Scott 2016, 12; Turner 2006, 127). Brand himself was supporting plans for "technoecological" colonies in outer space, even funding space colonization research with royalties from his catalog (Anker 2005, 240). The terminology used to describe these colonies was especially important to Brand, who was advocating against the term "space settlements."

> Speaking of terms, the use of the term 'Space Colony' has been expressly forbidden by the US State Department because of anti-colonial feelings around the world. So NASA has shrugged and adopted 'Space Settlements'—unpoetic terminology since the last thing you do in Space is settle. We're sticking to 'Space Colonies.' It's more accurate; this time there's a difference in that no Space natives are being

colonized; and the term reminds us of things that went badly and went well in previous colonizations. If we're lucky we may enact a parallel with what happened in Europe when America was being colonized. Intellectual ferment - new lands meant new possibilities; new possibilities meant new ideas. (Brand 1977, 5)

[Fig. 3] *Space Colonies* revolves around O'Neill's vision, containing contributions to the debate of space colonization (Source: Amazon)

As biologist Danielle Lee states, the vocabulary used to describe the dream of colonizing Mars is based on imagery of imperial colonialism (2015a; 2015b). Beyond that, it is depicting the heroicness of male colonizers who conquered and organized the chaotic, unknown, dangerous and wild continents, often drawing parallels of the fertility of the land with that of Indigenous women (Blunt & Rose 1994, 8–14). The distinction between chaotic nature and orderly (space) technology runs along intersecting colonial and patriarchal lines (Mies 1998, 77). Gerard Kitchen O'Neill, a physicist and name giver of the space settlement concept the "O'Neill cylinder", based his visions on the frontier myth that came with the first European settlements on the American continent and whose "function is to provide a historical account and an ideological justification of national development, and a repertoire of exemplary fables … that explain and justify the development of American nationality as the product of this perennial advance into the wilderness, or the 'virgin land'" (Slotkin 2015, 1). This frontier myth also appealed to John Allen, leading figure in the story of Synergia Ranch and *Biosphere 2*, who "considered himself a son of the Western frontier" (Reider 2009, 18). In the 1975 Fall issue of *The CoEvolution Quarterly*, another editorship of Stewart Brand that grew out of the *Supplement to the Whole Earth Catalog*, O'Neill writes: "The human race stands now on the threshold of a new frontier, whose richness surpasses a thousand fold that of the new western world of five hundred years ago" (O'Neill 1978, 209). At this time, O'Neill worked on designing space habitats with his students at Princeton University and his well-known book *The High Frontier: Human Colonies in Space*, in which he envisioned space colonies as suburban, middle-class, liberal communities much like a new "America in the skies" (Kilgore 2003, 156–168; Turner 2006, 126).

According to Anker, "space colonies came to represent rational, orderly, and wise management, in contrast to the irrational, disorderly, and ill-managed Earth. Some of them built Biosphere 2 in Arizona to prepare for colonization of Mars and to create a model for how life on Earth should be organized" (2005, 240). In this context, *Biosphere 2* figures as a topos illustrating the relation between ecosystem science, counterculture, space flight, and colonial expansion. It contains not only the beliefs and cultural motifs of a time in which the Cold War nuclear arms race and environmental activism culminated in apocalyptic imaginings of a near future. The case of *Biosphere 2* additionally displays the "Western" modern desire to create a technologically enhanced and controlled second nature that is fundamentally and materially linked with colonial exploitation, ultimately unfolding how "Western" utopias are unconceivable without the history of colonialism and misogyny.[3]

D(o)omed to Fail

In the same year as the *Earthrise* photographs were taken, the microbiologist Clair Folsome filled a flask with Pacific Ocean water (including invisible microorganisms), sand, algae and a crayfish and sealed the container. He observed this ensemble in his lab and found that "[w]ithout any interaction or exposure to the exterior air, the microscopic world of sea life inside survived many cycles of photosynthetic and metabolic exchanges" (Miller 2011, 105). Folsome called this ensemble an "ecosphere," characterizing a miniaturized enclosed system that preserves living conditions for the contained organisms (Miller 2011, 105; Lévêque 2003, 75). With this experiment, the vision of a capsular autonomous ecosystem and the "phantasm of a change of media without changing media" (Wessely 2013, 137; my translation) became more probable.[4] When the glass dome architecture of *Biosphere 2* was conceptualized, Folsome joined the project, giving insight into his small-scale ecosphere research and advising "the Biosphere 2 designers that they could collect air and water from

3 A look back into the history of closed ecosystems reveals another entanglement with colonialism. So-called plant cabins or Wardian cages invented by physician and botany enthusiast Nathaniel Bagshaw Ward allowed exotic plants from overseas to be transferred to European states in the nineteenth century (Vennen 2018, 35–62; Ward [1842] 2013).

4 Nathaniel Bagshaw Ward happened to make the same discovery in 1829 when he accidentally left a flask on his windowsill, which he had used to observe butterfly caterpillars beforehand. After a couple of days, small plants began to spring inside the corked bottle that was covered with leaves and soil. After his discovery of this microclimate inside the bottle, he even began to construct experimental houses that were "attached to the greenhouse, the largest of which was over seven meters long, three and a half meters wide and almost three meters high. A wide variety of climates, from alpine to tropical regions, should be united under one and the same (glass) roof." (Vennen 2018, 44; my translation).

 anywhere they wanted in the world; no matter what, the microbiota would work out a way to maintain the system. Life forms would evolve their own equilibrium at every level" (Reider 2009, 114).[5] These self-sustaining ecospheres not only resonate with *Biosphere 2* but also symbolically with the *Earthrise* photographs, as both fueled "a new holistic paradigm" (Sattler 2017, 376).

[Fig. 4] Clair Folsome with one of his ecospheres (Source: Nelson 2019, 10)

When the first enclosure experiment in *Biosphere 2* started, the interweaving of ecosphere and space mission research became strikingly obvious: the eight biospherians were dressed in dark blue space suits and bid farewell in a grand ceremony like astronauts.[6] Historian of science Sabine Höhler (2016, 125) found that the chosen number of eight crew members was due to earlier space exploration research, as it was suggested to be the

5 Folsome was introduced to Allen and Nelson by Lynn Margulis at the Cosmos Conference in 1983 (Munns & Nickelsen 2017, 289).

6 These future biospherians were previously subjected to psychological tests to assess their suitability for the experiment. It is noteworthy that all biospherians fit into the so-called psychological '"adventurer"' profile, being highly sociable, active, and less prone to depression than others (Reider 2009, 136; Nelson 2019, 204).

optimum amount of people for a crewed mission to Mars. After the two years of enclosure, Jane Poynter and Taber MacCallum, both scientists of the first mission, reported that they developed a similar sense of deep attachment and reverence to their environment that Schweikart described when seeing Earth from space, also called the "Overview Effect" (Klotz 2014). The architecture of *Biosphere 2* supported this emotional impression, as it was constructed according to cabin-ecology parameters. It contained a general life-support system, similar to the design that was established by Eugene Odum in 1963 at the Princeton Conferences on *Human Ecology in Space Flight*. This life-support system was mainly managed by what the biospherians have referred to as the "technosphere," the background technology, which was located in its basement. The term was originally introduced by the control engineer John H. Milsum in the late 1960s and recently gained popularity in the Anthropocene discourse owing to Peter Haff's adoption of it.[7] In the case of *Biosphere 2* the life-supporting "technosphere" consists of structures for water regulation and air circulation as well as heating and cooling systems (Allen, Alling, and Nelson 2003, 1633). As cultural historian Benjamin Bühler asserts, this "'life support system' was to grant future space travelers total material autonomy from Earth" (2012, 187; my translation). To construct this life-support system is simultaneously to construct nature as infrastructure, channeling

7 Haff (2013, 301f.) defines the technosphere as "the set of large-scale networked technologies that underlie and make possible rapid extraction from the Earth of large quantities of free energy and subsequent power generation, long-distance, nearly instantaneous communication, rapid long-distance energy and mass transport, the existence and operation of modern governmental and other bureaucracies, high-intensity industrial and manufacturing operations including regional, continental and global distribution of food and other goods, and a myriad additional 'artificial' or 'non-natural' processes without which modern civilization and its present 7 × 10 human constituents could not exist."

 those properties and materials that seem suitable. At the same time, to construct the system is also to create its failure.[8]

After a couple of months, the life-support system of *Biosphere* 2 seemed inefficient, because numerous organisms had already been adversely affected by life within the dome. All pollinating insects and some vertebrate species died, human occupants were tormented by fatigue, plants withered, trees rotted, the corals in the artificial ocean were stunted, and crops failed (Reider 2009, 162; Broad 1996). What triggered these developments was a significant decrease in the oxygen concentration (Nelson 2019, 174–84). In order to fix this, the glass house was repeatedly supplied with external oxygen, which broke the planned isolation of the system. Some believed that the oxygen was absorbed by the concrete the hills were made of, and that it diffused faster than CO2 through the glass shell (Dempster 1999, 36f.). One year after the end of the first experiment, several crew members, in collaboration with other scientists, published a paper that linked oxygen depletion with high levels of microbial respiration (Severinghaus et al. 1994, 35–37). To put it simply, their thesis was that so much organic material was distributed in such a small space, that the oxygen was just not enough for everyone. The consequences, however, were serious: the atmospheric equilibrium within the dome was disturbed and the crew suffered from sleep apnea. In turn, this induced stress likely contributed to inner-group conflicts that led to a division into two groups. One was committed to the original goal of ensuring complete enclosure, which was welcomed and supported by project management (Reider 2009, 188f.). The other group proposed loosening the closure of the ecosystem, at least piecewise, and importing food, allowing more time for scientific research. The latter argued that the farming of their fields and maintenance of their animals consumed too much time. The departure of a crew

8 Florian Sprenger remarks "The failure is inscribed to these projects because they try to create an ecosystem without an environment in an environment" (Sprenger 2019, 452, my translation).

member due to an injury and her re-entry into the dome with various new things—it was rumored that the two plastic bags she took in contained fast food—resulted in negative media coverage (Nelson 2019, 201f.). In addition, food was in short supply: the scientists even began to eat the seeds that they had been due to plant (Poynter 2006, 147; Reider 2009, 155).

As a composition of different organisms from different regions across the globe—on the basis of Folsome's insight—the glazed and domed heterotopian space of *Biosphere 2* figures as a hybrid ecology that simulates naturalness through regulating and controlling "nature" while simultaneously naturalizing it. What was suggested as an exact and controllable composition of biota proved to be a practically ambiguous, insubordinate and non-determinable mixture of organisms and substances. Ultimately "[t]he act of enclosing and detaining nature in an exceptional space made the 'natural state' reappear—a state of nature the biospherians believed to have harnessed and mastered" (Höhler 2010, 51). From the human perspective, these developments add up to a failed experiment. Nevertheless, these conditions, which have proven disastrous for many species, were ideal for other organisms, especially cockroaches and ants (Wetterer et al. 1999).

Shifting Perspectives

The story of *Biosphere 2* shows that, on our way to space, we could literally lose the air we breathe. The experiment stands as the embodiment of the ideology of closed cybernetic systems married with the ideas of expansion, never ending growth, and colonialism, with the addendum that "no space natives are being colonized"—only inanimate matter like the high-iron red dust on the surface on Mars. I argue that this is only a partial narrative of the experiment and will continue interrogating its blind spots. Who is addressed as agent, who is not? Whose perspective is shown, whose is not? These are the same questions that were raised against the Anthropocene concept by feminist theorists like Donna J. Haraway (2016) and Kathryn Yusoff (2018). In posing these questions, they call attention to definitory power, economical hierarchies, and the systematic exclusion of other perspectives and voices. It is in this manner that I read the following statement by evolutionary biologist Lynn Margulis:

> Humans, if someday they trek in giant spaceships to other planets, will not be alone. In space as on Earth, the elements of life, carbon, oxygen, hydrogen, nitrogen, sulfur, and phosphorus and a few others, must recycle. This recycling is no suburban luxury; it is a principle of life from which no technology can deliver us. Human voyages into deep space require ecosystems composed of many nonhuman organisms to recycle waste into food. (Margulis 1999, 132)

Margulis was also a speaker at the Galactic Conference at Synergia Ranch in 1982 and in several ways associated with *Biosphere 2* and space colony research.[9] She allegedly predicted that the biomes in the artificial sphere would become "urban weed," i.e., plants and animals that "flourish in the edges of the patchwork habitats that people make" (Kelly 1994, 137). With Dorian Sagan she wrote the book *Biospheres From Earth to Space*, which advocated for building a closed ecosystem on Earth before building one on other planets. Margulis' interest in *Biosphere 2* seemed to be more directed to finding answers to how the Earth's ecosystem works. In a comment on O'Neill's visions for space colonies written for the *Space Colonies* Supplement to the *Whole Earth Catalog*, she states:

> Why do some sun-requiring algae actually live inside carbonate rocks? Why do you find small blind arthopods scurrying at the backs of caves? Why do giant luminescent female fish (carrying their tiny males parasitically) inhabit the abyss? Why do red and green microorganisms cover the

9 Margulis formulated the Gaia hypothesis together with James Lovelock in the 1970s. According to her, Gaia resembles interacting ecosystems rather than a single and whole organism (1999, 141–161).

> newly fallen arctic snows and multiply on its surface? Why do certain funny poorly known fungi (examples in the group Laboulgeniomycetes) live only on the left anterior appendage (read left front toe) of its insect host? The answer is the same as the one to the question why do people like O'Neill and his students imagine Space Colonies and advocate the move out. (Margulis 1977)[10]

The non-human agents Margulis addresses were the ones spreading fear of possible "back-contamination" when the US Apollo missions to the moon began (Compton 1989). Recent research has shown that the International Space Station (ISS) is not only carrying human beings in a supposedly sterile environment: "The results reveal a diverse population of bacteria and fungi on ISS environmental surfaces that changed over time but remained similar between locations. The dominant organisms are associated with the human microbiome" (Checinska Sielaff et al. 2019). Thinking that the evolution of ecological systems can be anticipated in terms of calculability and autopoiesis, the extensive interdependencies and entanglements living beings are involved in are remaining blind spots. Space colonization is not a microbial desire—it presents itself as a human fantasy of rational order that, as media theorist Sarah Sharma pointed out, is itself "an exercise of patriarchal power, a privilege that occurs at the expense of cultivating and sustaining conditions of collective autonomy" (2017). If indeed *Biosphere 2* is seen as a failure of this fantasy, it therefore offers itself as a breeding ground for telling another story.

The Vitruvian Ant

To not only reproduce this narrative of failure but to go further in uncovering its epistemic assumptions that are yet invisible I want

10 At the end of the article, Margulis poses the crucial question "If we invest in Space Colonies from what other budget lines do we take the funds?" (1977).

[Fig. 5] A tardigrade or "water-bear," a microscopic organism that accidentally made its way to the Moon, presumably dormant (Source: Scanning electron micrograph by Bob Goldstein & Vicky Madden, distributed under a CC-BY 2.0 license)

to outline another possible perspective. In order to re-narrate the story of *Biosphere 2*, I propose a shift in focus onto alliances and transitions that exceed the story of so-called distinct, passive, and operable factors. I will center the perspective of those organisms, which surpassed the glass walls and revealed whose agency has been left out. In doing so, I am following Haraway's approach of using "string figures as a theoretical trope, a way to think-with a host of companions in sympoietic threading, felting, tangling, tracking, and sorting" (2016, 31). What shatters the glass dome is the appearance of those organisms that ate their way through the glass ball, settled in it, made it permeable, composted it, and thus composed another perspective on this story. To understand this perspective, we need to follow the cockroaches and the ants.

Four different kinds of cockroaches were deliberately imported into *Biosphere 2* to recycle organic waste. The common household cockroach, although not one of them, was the most prevalent species in the glass dome and the population of this "great evolutionary survivor" (Nelson 2018b), as ecologist and former biospherian Mark Nelson dubbed it, nearly exploded. Dating back to the Jurassic period, the species' longevity comes as no surprise regarding their collective knowing and doing, their ecology of practices: first, they are outstanding recyclers, eating almost every organic waste material; second, gregarious cockroaches display collective decision-making when searching for food or shelter; and third, cockroaches have the ability to adapt to almost every environment:

> [T]he social biology of domiciliary cockroaches so far can be characterised by a common shelter, overlapping generations, non-closure of groups, equal reproductive potential of group members, an absence of task specialisation, high levels of social dependence, central place foraging, social information transfer, kin recognition, and a meta-population structure. (Lihoreau, Costa, and Rivault 2012)

The ants, however, made their way into *Biosphere 2* by eating five holes through the sealed glass dome. More specifically, it was *Paratrechina longicornis*, also baptized "crazy ant" because of its erratic movements. This ant species lives in symbiosis with scale insects. These so-called plant pests feed on tree sap and excrete honeydew. The ants use the honeydew as food, so they protect the scale insects from their predators and support them in their spreading (Wetterer et al. 1999, 386). One could argue against my point that the ants tell us a different story, because they are organized in colonies and act altruistically due to their queen, who controls the entire population. However, biologist Deborah Gordon has shown that the ant queen is not—as is often assumed—a "cybernetic super brain" that manages all processes within the ant colony. Rather, ants are organized in task groups whose size and affiliation vary according to the importance of the task (Gordon 2010, 45–74). In this sense, the ants inhabiting *Biosphere 2* were much better organized than the human bio-spherians. The division of the eight scientists into two hostile groups evolved due to their relation to project management—as opponents or advocates. Artists Hito Steyerl and Anton Vidokle frame the situation as follows: "the ants especially had great social tactics, they practiced a form of cross-colony solidarity, which made them very resilient. The humans just divided and fell out; of course the ants won" (Steyerl & Vidokle 2017).

The crazy ant is categorized as "tramp ant" as it is present around the globe, "dispersed worldwide by human commerce and associated with human disturbance" (Wetterer et al. 1999, 384). Seen this way, the ants are closely linked to human agency and history. By focusing on organisms that invaded *Biosphere 2*, I am aiming to reflect the inherent anthropocentrism of the experiment and to irritate a standardized default anthropocentric view that situates "nature" as the "other", as the unknown, wild, chaotic "virgin" land that is feminized and racialized and that can and needs to be controlled and managed. The feminization of land, nature and the Earth as a nurturing mother or a wicked stepmother has a long tradition in Western thought. It builds upon the modern classification of nature and women as passive and subordinate (Merchant 1990, 1–41). It is also connected to imperial imagery that sexualizes the space to be colonized, indeed drawing a parallel of colonial and sexual control over Indigenous women (Blunt & Rose 1994, 10).

Contextualizing the *Biosphere 2* story and looking at its entanglements from different perspectives is a way of research inspired by historian of science Carolyn Merchant's take on feminist history:

> Feminist history in the broadest sense requires that we look at history with egalitarian eyes, seeing it anew from the viewpoint not only of women but also of social and racial groups and the natural environment, previously ignored as the underlying resources on which Western culture and its progress have been built. To write history from a feminist perspective is to turn it upside down—to see social structure from the bottom up. (1990, xx)

Accordingly, I want to suggest a provocative experiment of thought by not thinking *like* or *as* but thinking *with* the ants: Are crazy ants stowaways of human globalized transport or did humans build this infrastructure unwittingly to enable crazy ants to travel globally? What if *Biosphere 2* is regarded as a shiny warm castle built for ants and cockroaches? What is the term "Ant-hropocene" really hinting at?

The view from the bottom up, from a creepy-crawlies' perspective, revolves around the ants and cockroaches who found a way to break the closed design of the ecosystem and establish themselves as unknown factors under the glass dome. Despite all efforts to include and regulate all factors of the biosphere experiment, these organisms managed to contaminate the isolated glass sphere. The attempt to build an autonomous system failed when viewed from the anthropocentric position that, in the case of *Biosphere 2*, sets the default human as one looking from "Extraterrestria" or from Sirius. From a creepy-crawlies' perspective, the idea of an autonomous, independent, separated system of human existence is shaken, as is the idea of "[b]ounded (or neoliberal) individualism amended by autopoiesis" (Haraway 2016, 33). Letting ants, cockroaches and other "muddy" organisms crawl into the human vantage point is a metaphorical take in order to think-with disruptive organisms, the agency of the excluded, and the impure mixtures. What this perspective hints at and what it is deeply entangled with is the idea of sympoiesis, carefully worded by scholar in environmental planning Beth Dempster (2000), who uses the term for collectively producing systems lacking centralized control and self-defined boundaries that are constantly changing and evolving. Sympoiesis implies challenging the imaginary of closed systems and boundaries as exemplified in the biospheric venture that aimed to separate a distinct ecosystem, thus only allowing humanly controlled biome compositions. In contrast, practicing symbiosis implies tentacular thinking, as well as cultivating care and response-ability that is always with, thinking-with, acting-with, worlding-with, creating laboratories of mud with regard to our entanglements and interspecies connections on this planet, and re-narrating stories, because "it matters what stories we tell, to tell other stories with" (Haraway 2016, 12).

A Rehearsal of the Anthropocene

To re-narrate the story of *Biosphere 2* and to change the focus of narration implies situating and contextualizing the knots and lines of flight that compose it. Following a creepy-crawlies' perspective not only decenters anthropocentric stories about *Biosphere 2* but also—on a methodological level—implies contamination and expansion of the boundaries of the story itself. Tracing the experiment in regard to its disturbances reveals its multiple enmeshments in colonial history, Western counterculture utopias, and space flight. At the same time, it lays bare modern conceptions of gender, ecosystems science, and ecology and evolutionary science, as well as contributing to a media history of environmental knowledge. From this perspective, the epistemic assumptions underlying the glass dome can be unearthed and challenged. Höhler outlines this in her concise remark, that "Biosphere 2 made a normative statement as to what purpose nature should serve at the turn of the twenty-first century, and for whom" (2010, 51). If *Biosphere 2* is indeed regarded as a performative "[r]ehearsal of the Anthropocene" (Sattler 2017, 379), the similarity of frictions and conflicts in this specific place can be seen revolving around the power of defining, naming, and telling stories. Likewise, this rehearsal indicated who is chosen to be an actor: In the words of biospherian Sally Silverstone, these were "essentially white middle-class, upper-middle class Western individuals who had never been short of food in their whole life" (Reider 2009, 154).

To point to those stories that underlie the major narrative is firstly to render it visible as a default narrative and secondly to introduce marginalized perspectives and voices. Telling different stories then enables other imaginings to become imaginable. Coming from creepy-crawlies and impure mixtures, *Biosphere 2* is a laboratory for examining the grounds of "Western" modern science, utopias, and laboratories themselves. It thus shifts the focus to interdependencies and sympoietic entanglements that can themselves be conceptualized as forms and practices of knowledge. Seen this way, it would be a useful method to discuss the concept of the Anthropocene, shifting the perspective to those voices and agencies that contaminate and irritate the discourse, opening up possibilities to reflect and change the default settings of knowledge production.

I would like to thank Réka, Lola, and Jakob for encouraging me to write - often without them even knowing it.

References

Allen, John. 2000. "The Whole Earth." *Visions Of Technology: A Century Of Vital Debate About Machines Systems and the Human World*, edited by Richard Rhodes, 264f. New York: Simon & Schuster.

Allen, John, Mark Nelson, and Tango Parrish. 1984. "Institute of Ecotechnics." *The Environmentalist* 4 (3): 205–18.

Allen, John, Mark Nelson, and Abigail Alling. 2003. "The legacy of Biosphere 2 for the study of biospherics and closed ecological systems." *Advances in Space Research* 31: 1629–39.

Anker, Peder. 2005. "The Ecological Colonization of Space." *Environmental History* 10: 239–68.

Blunt, Allison, and Gillian Rose, eds. 1994. *Writing Women and Space: Colonial and Postcolonial Geographies*, New York: Guilford Press.

Brand, Stewart. 1977. "The Sky Starts at Your Feet." In *Space Colonies*, edited by Stewart Brand. Accessed March 30, 2020. https://settlement.arc.nasa.gov/CoEvolutionBook/p2.html.

Broad, William. 1986. "Ultimate Survival: Desert Dreamers Build a Man Made World." *The New York Times*, May 27. Accessed December 15, 2020. https://www.nytimes.com/1986/05/27/science/ultimate-survival-desert-dreamers-build-a-man-made-world.html.

Broad, William. 1991. "As Biosphere Is Sealed, Its Patron Reflects on Life." *The New York Times*, September 24. Accessed December 15, 2020. https://www.nytimes.com/1991/09/24/science/as-biosphere-is-sealed-its-patron-reflects-on-life.html.

Broad, William. 1996. "Paradise Lost: Biosphere Retooled as Atmospheric Nightmare." *The New York Times*, November 19. Accessed December 15, 2020. https://www.nytimes.com/1996/11/19/science/paradise-lost-biosphere-retooled-as-atmospheric-nightmare.html.

Bühler, Benjamin. 2012. "Entgleitende Regulierungen: Zukunftsfiktionen der Politischen Ökologie." *Selbstläufer / Leerläufer: Regelungen und ihr Imaginäres im 20. Jahrhundert*, edited by Stefan Rieger, 177–97. Zürich: diaphanes.

Calloway, Doris Howes, ed. 1966. *Human Ecology in Spaceflight: Proceedings of the First International Interdisciplinary Conference*. New York: The New York Academy of Sciences.

Checinska Sielaff, Aleksandra, Camilla Urbaniak, Ganesh Babu Malli Mohan, et al. 2019. "Characterization of the Total and Viable Bacterial and Fungal Communities Associated with the International Space Station Surfaces." *Microbiome* 7: 50. doi.org/10.1186/s40168-019-0666-x.

Compton, David. 1989. *Where No Man Has Gone Before: A History of Apollo Lunar Exploration Missions*. [Published as NASA Special Publication-4214 in the NASA History Series.] Accessed March 30, 2020. https://www.hq.nasa.gov/office/pao/History/SP-4214/contents.html.

Dempster, Ruth. 2000. "Sympoietic and Autopoietic Systems: A New Distinction for Self-Organizing Systems." Accessed March 30, 2020. https://pdfs.semanticscholar.org/4429/9317a20afcd33b0a11d3b2bf4fc196088d45.pdf.

Dempster, William. 1999. "Biosphere 2 Engineering Design." *Ecological Engineering* 13 (1): 31–42.

Franke, Anselm. 2013. "Earthrise and the Disappearance of the Outside." In *The Whole Earth: California and the Disappearance of the Outside*, edited by Anselm Franke and Diedrich Diederichsen, 12–19. Berlin: Sternberg Press.

Fuller, R. Buckminster. 1968. "City of the Future." *PLAYBOY* 15 (1): 166–168; 228–230.

Fuller, R. Buckminster. (1969) 2017. *Operating Manual for Spaceship Earth*. Zürich: Lars Müller Publishers.

Gordon, Deborah. 2010. *Ant Encounters. Interaction Networks and Colony Behavior.* Princeton, NJ: Princeton University Press.

Haff, Peter. 2013. "Technology as a geological phenomenon: implications for human well-being." *Geological Society London*, Special Publications, 395 (1): 301–309.

Haraway, Donna J. 2016. *Staying With the Trouble.* Durham, NC: Duke University Press.

Höhler, Sabine. 2010. "The Environment as a Life Support System: The Case of Biosphere 2." *History and Technology* 26 (1): 39–58.

Höhler, Sabine. 2016. *Spaceship Earth in the Environmental Age, 1960–1990.* London: Routledge.

Institute of Ecotechnics. "1982 Galactic Conference." *Institute of Ecotechnics*, September 17. Accessed 04 January, 2021. https://ecotechnics.edu/project/1982-conference/.

Kavka, Misha. 2012. *Reality TV.* Edinburgh: Edinburgh University Press.

Kelly, Kevin. 1994. *Out Of Control: The New Biology of Machines, Social Systems and the Economic World.* Accessed 30 March, 2020. http://library.uniteddiversity.coop/More_Books_and_Reports/OutOfControlNewBiologyOfMachinesSocialSystemsAndEconomicWorld.pdf.

Kilgore, De Witt Douglas. 2003. *Astrofuturism: Science, Race, and Visions of Utopia in Space.* Philadelphia: University of Pennsylvania Press.

Klotz, Irene. 2014. "Jane Poynter and Taber MacCallum, Co-founders, Paragon Space Development Corp." *Space News*, January 6. Accessed March 30, 2020. https://spacenews.

com/38952profile-jane-poynter-and-taber-maccallum-co-founders-paragon-space-development/.

Latour, Bruno. 2018. *Down to Earth: Politics in the New Climatic Regime*, translated by Catherine Porter. Medford, MA: Polity Press.

Lee, Danielle. 2015a. "Colonize Mars? Not Until We Learn Some Lessons here on Earth." *Splinter*, May 4. Accessed March 30, 2020. https://splinternews.com/colonize-mars-not-until-we-learn-some-lessons-here-on-1793847525.

Lee, Danielle. 2015b. "When Discussing Humanity's Next Move to Space, the Language We Use Matters." *Scientific American*, March 26. Accessed March 30, 2020. https://blogs.scientificamerican.com/urban-scientist/when-discussing-humanity-8217-s-next-move-to-space-the-language-we-use-matters/.

Lévêque, Christian. 2003. *Ecology: From Ecosystem to Biosphere.* Enfield, NH: Science Publishers.

Lihoreau, Mathieu, J. T. Costa, and Colette Rivault. 2012. "The Social Biology of Domiciliary Cockroaches: Colony Structure, Kin Recognition and Collective Decisions." *Insectes Sociaux* 59 (4): 445–52.

Margulis, Lynn. 1977. "Comment on O'Neill's Space Colonies." In *Space Colonies*, edited by Stewart Brand. Accessed March 30, 2020. https://settlement.arc.nasa.gov/CoEvolutionBook/DEBATE.HTML#LYNN%20MARGULIS.

Margulis, Lynn. 1999. *The Symbiotic Planet. A New Look at Evolution.* London: Phoenix.

Merchant, Carolyn. 1990. *The Death of Nature: Women, Ecology and the Scientific Revolution*. San Francisco: Harper & Row.

Mies, Maria. 1998. *Patriarchy and Accumulation on a World Scale: Women in the International Division of Labour.* London: Zed Books.

Mignano, Mitch. 2015. "From the Archive: R. Buckminster Fuller at the 1982 Galactic Conference." *Synergetic Press*. February 12. Accessed March 30, 2020. https://www.synergeticpress.com/images-synergetic-archive/.

Miller, Meredith. 2011. "SPHERES, DOMES, LIMITS, INTERFACES. The Transgressive Architecture of Biosphere 2." In *Where Do You Stand? ACSA Annual Meeting Proceedings*, edited by Alberto Perez-Gomez, Anne Comier, and Annie Pedret, 102–110. Washington, DC: ACSA Press.

Munns, David P. D. & Nickelsen, Kärin. 2017. "To Live Among the Stars: Artificial Environments in the Early Space Age." *History and Technology* 33 (3). 272–299.

Nelson, Mark. 2018a. "Some Ecological and Human Lessons of Biosphere 2." *European Journal of Ecology* 4 (1): 50–55.

Nelson, Mark. 2018b. "Out of This World." *Dartmouth Alumni Magazine*, May 1, 44–49.

Nelson, Mark. 2019. *Pushing Our Limits: Insights from Biosphere 2*. Tucson: University of Arizona Press.

Niller, Eric. 2016. "Trump's Chief Strategist Steve Bannon Ran a Massive Climate Experiment." *Wired*, July 12. Accessed March 30, 2020. https://www.wired.com/2016/12/trumps-chief-strategist-ran-massive-climate-experiment/.

O'Neill, Gerard. 1977. "The High Frontier." In *Space Colonies. A CoEvolution Book*, edited by Stewart Brand. Accessed January 04, 2021. https://space.nss.org/settlement/nasa/CoEvolutionBook/HIGHF.html

O'Neill, Gerard. 1978. "Space Colonies" In *Shelter II*, edited by Lloyd Kahn and Bob Easton, 209–211. Bolinas, CA: Shelter Publications.

Odum, Eugene Pleasants, and Gary W. Barrett. (1953) 1971. *Fundamentals of Ecology*. Boston, MA: Thomson Brooks/Cole.

Poynter, Jane. 2006. *The Human Experiment: Two Years and Twenty Minutes Inside Biosphere 2*. New York: Thunder's Mouth Press.

Reider, Rebecca. 2009. *Dreaming the Biosphere: The Theater of All Possibilities*. Albuquerque: University of New Mexiko Press.

Sattler, Meredith. 2017. "Boundaries and Frontiers at Biosphere 2: 1991–1994." In *Architecture of Complexity: Design, Systems, Society and Environment*, edited by Ryan E. Smith, Keith Diaz Moore, and Windy Zhao, 372–82. Salt Lake City: University of Utah, College of Architecture and Planning.

Scott, Felicity. 2016. *Outlaw Territories: Environments of Insecurity/Architectures of Counterinsurgency*. New York: Zone Books.

Severinghaus, Jeffrey P., Wallace S. Broecker, William F. Dempster, Taber MacCallum, and Martin Wahlen. 1994. "Oxygen Loss in Biosphere 2." *EOS* 75 (3): 33–40.

Sharma, Sarah. 2017. "Exit and the Extensions of Man." *transmediale*. May 8. Accessed March 30, 2020. https://transmediale.de/content/exit-and-the-extensions-of-man.

Slotkin, R. 2015. "Myth of the Frontier". *The Wiley Blackwell Encyclopedia of Race, Ethnicity, and Nationalism*, edited by J. Stone et al. 1–4. Hoboken, NJ: Wiley.

Sprenger, Florian. 2019. *Epistemologien des Umgebens: Zur Geschichte, Ökologie und Biopolitik künstlicher Environments*. Bielefeld: transcript.

Steyerl, Hito, and Anton Vidokle. 2017. "Cosmic Catwalk and the Production of Time." *e-flux* 82. Accessed March 30, 2020. https://www.e-flux.com/journal/82/134989/cosmic-catwalk-and-the-production-of-time/.

Turner, Fred. 2006. *From Counterculture to Cyberculture*. Chicago: University of Chicago Press.

Vennen, Mareike. 2018. *Das Aquarium: Praktiken, Techniken und Medien der Wissensproduktion (1840–1910)*. Göttingen: Wallstein Verlag.

Ward, Nathaniel Bagshaw. (1842) 2013. On The Growth of Plants in Closely Glazed Cases. Cambridge: Cambridge University Press.

Wessely, Christina. 2013. "Wässrige Milieus. Ökologische Perspektiven in Meeresbiologie und Aquarienkunde um 1900." *Berliner Wissenschaftsgeschichte* 36: 128–47.

Wetterer, J. K., S. E. Miller, D. E. Wheeler, et al. 1999. "Ecological Dominance by *Paratrechina longicornis* (Hymenoptera: Formicidae), an Invasive Tramp Ant, in Biosphere 2." *The Florida Entomologist* 82 (3): 381–88.

Yusoff, Kathryn. 2018. *A Billion Black Anthropocenes or None*. Minneapolis: University of Minnesota Press.

Zabel, Peter. 1996. "The Biosphere 2 experiment." *Telepolis*, April 29. Accessed March 30, 2020. https://www.heise.de/tp/features/The-Biosphere-2-experiment-3445905.html.

Oktopus

Kinga Tóth

Those of us who have stayed and have
changed try to cling to what we've mastered,
we grow a membrane and learn to swim, to
touch, to stroke other skin still shedding,
we're not slimy enough yet, but our fins are
growing between our fingers, our hair wavier
in the new substance. The salt corrodes the
eyeballs, then, as the lungs pass suffocation,
the fins relax, the edemata relax, this is the
post-apocalypse Atlantis, where the plant-
animal-human remains build love relations.
We are light, like old air balloons, we carry
one another's weight, we understand one
another's polyglot, our crowns receive into
ourselves, at night we intertwine our limbs,
when the air bubbles of the old town fall, the
high tide gathers up the years of nylon bags,
while using our fluids we glue them into a
large curtain, swimming multi-limbed homo
piscarius, this is our night. With our index
arms we throw our one self, dancing halfway
up to the upper strata we manage to hold
together, till now unsuccessful, landed with
the new breath.

Translated by Owen Good

SUBMARINE INFRASTRUCTURES

MARINE ECOLOGY

NUCLEAR TEST SITES

DEEP-SEA MINING

CORAL REEFS

COLONIZATION

[7]

Colonizing the Ocean: Coral Reef Histories in the Anthropocene

Petra Löffler

This article analyzes historical and current attempts to colonize the ocean. Each section discusses different, but interrelated, geopolitical strategies of colonization: first, I focus on the occupation of a territory and its marine environment by military means, turning it into a site of environmental degradation—a "debrisphere." I discuss the series of nuclear tests, conducted by the US military in the 1950s on Bikini Atoll, as stratigraphic traces of the Anthropocene. Second, I examine the exploitation of deep-sea resources in the form of the extraction of oil or gas from the seafloor, as well as the removal of corals and other sediments from reefs to collect, analyze, store and display in museums. I argue that these operations share the same interest

of possessing marine resources. Third, I analyze utopias as well as scientific programs aiming to populate submarine environments. In all sections I posit that keeping in mind the world-building yet fragile ecology of coral reefs is important for critical accounts of the Anthropocene. They show how endangered multi-species habitats are in times of anthropogenic extraction, pollution, and global warming.

> The sea holds the great resources of nature. It is through the sea that life began, so to speak, and who knows if it will not end there!
> *Jules Verne*

> The ocean remembers.
> *Robert Kandel*

A Diffractive Mapping of the Ocean

In the following I will trace the deep time history and ecology of coral reefs by relating the Pacific Ocean and the Caribbean Sea. In connecting concrete sites and historical events that have taken place in one geographical area or another at varying times, I understand the ocean both as a diachronic meshwork of currents of knowledge production—an epistemic milieu—and as a geopolitically contested and colonized space. I will dive deeply into the natural and cultural history of the ocean, focusing on coral reef communities. Transversing their marine geology, geography, and biology will allow me to hone in on technologies and practices developed for the exploration of these seemingly strange realms. Western sciences have a close relationship with the politics of space—as David Livingstone (2003, 180) put it, knowledge production has its own geographies: the laboratory as the space of manipulation, the field as the space of expedition, the museum as the space of presentation, and the archive as the space of circulation. In the Anthropocene histories of corals and coral reefs, all of these geographies are entangled. The long-term and intricate prominence of corals and coral reefs in the natural sciences and beyond, and the alliance of these sciences with Western colonial politics, will guide the reader through the sections, showing their many facets in *diffractions* (Barad 2007). A diffractive reading of these intertwined stories has the advantage of connecting oneself to diverse and sometimes contradictory histories, which allows the reader to grapple with complex yet urgent questions regarding anthropogenic extraction and climatic politics.

11° 37′ N, 165° 24′ E: Bikini Atoll—Nuclear Tests, Stratigraphic Traces and System Ecology

Able, Baker, Union, Yankee, Flathead, Dakota, Fir, Nutmeg, Sycamore, Maple, Aspen, Redwood, Hickory, Cedar, Poplar, Juniper—these are some of the names of the bombs that the US military detonated in the lagoon of Bikini Atoll between June 30, 1946 and July 22, 1958, most of them underwater. Other bombs were released on Namu and Eninman, two of a totality of 26 islands of the atoll located in the northern Pacific Ocean. Three islands were vaporized during the bombing: Bokonijien, Aerokojlol, and Nam. On February 28, 1954 the US military detonated an immense hydrogen bomb named Bravo on the island of Nam, which was a thousand times more powerful than the atomic bombs dropped on Hiroshima and Nagasaki in 1945. The detonation, which left a huge crater replacing the island, not only contaminated people on the surrounding islands and neighboring inhabited atolls, but also the fishermen who were at sea that day.

Over a period of more than 10 years, Bikini Atoll and Eniwetok Atoll became the sites of a series of mostly submarine nuclear tests, making them uninhabitable to the Ri Majõl, how the Mashallese people call themselves, and highly toxic to plants, animals, and marine life. It is therefore all the more disturbing that the last 10 bombs deployed in the lagoon of Bikini Atoll between 11 May and 22 July, 1958 during Operation Hardtack bear the names of well-known trees in North America and beyond. Even more alienating is the fact that other bombs used during the US military nuclear tests were given the names of Indigenous North American tribes. The choice of the remote and sparsely populated atolls as a nuclear test site not only ignored the rights of its Indigenous peoples, but also endangered the habitat, food, and shelter for many marine species.[1] This was no doubt a brutal act of colonization through both military power and nomenclature—but it was also a brutal act of violence on the ocean's most diverse habitats and some of the richest resources of our planet.[2]

Among geologists, detectable traces of nuclear weapon tests are widely discussed as evident events—a so-called global stratigraphic section and point (GSSP) or simply "golden spike"—to take as the beginning of the new epoch of the Anthropocene. In geology, a new epoch in Earth history—a "global standard stratigraphic age" (GSSA)—is determined through the

1 Niedenthal (2013) reports the colonial history of Bikini Atoll and the effects of the nuclear tests by the US military from the point of view of its Indigenous inhabitants.

2 Marine habitats are subdivided in correspondence to the depth of the sea, ranging from the littoral and intertidal zones through the pelagic and mesophotic zones to the deep sea and benthic zones. Naturalist Carl von Linné used the Latin term "habitat" in his 1753 treatise *Species Plantarum*—literally meaning "lives in."

measurement of a series of geologically relevant events, which can be read in the layers of the Earth or found in materials like wood, shells or ice, and which occur more or less synchronously all over the world. The spreading of artificial radionuclides since the first atomic bomb explosions in 1945 counts as such a globally recognizable signal (Zalasiewicz et al. 2015). With a half-life of more than 5,000 years, radioactive plutonium-239 in particular qualifies as a chronological marker for the Anthropocene stratal record. It will still be detectable in carbonaceous materials such as wood, shells or bones for 50,000 years. In this respect, corals also play an important part as high-resolution archives of plutonium-239, caesium-137, and carbon-14 radionuclides (Waters et al. 2019).

Between 1945 and 1998 more than 2,000 nuclear weapon tests were carried out, about three quarters underground or underwater, mainly in central Asia, the Pacific Ocean, and the western USA. Besides the fact that the "majority of anthropogenic sourced radionuclides present in the environment today were produced by atmospheric nuclear bomb tests" (Waters et al. 2019, 192), the nuclear fallout reaches the oceans and its many inhabitants, although always delayed. However, the first detonation of the Trinity A-bomb in Alamogordo, New Mexico, on July 16, 1945 was not what geologists regularly deem a stratigraphically decisive event. Rather, the focus is on the series of hydrogen bomb tests started by the USA in 1952 that produced significant global fallout signals. With the detonation of the hydrogen bomb *Bravo* on February 28, 1954, which destroyed the island of Nam—an event locally remembered as the "day of two suns"—an immense atomic precipitation contaminated the atmosphere and sea around Bikini Atoll.

Making the land as well as the ocean uninhabitable for people, land animals, and marine life ought to count as a violent act of colonization through resettlement and environmental degradation. Only in 1977 did the United Nations General Assembly forbid the "deliberate manipulation of natural processes—the dynamics, composition, or structure of the Earth, including its biota, lithosphere, hydrosphere and atmosphere, or outer space" (Bonneuil and Fressoz 2015, 128). At the same time, Marshallese people were fighting for a Nuclear Free and Independent Pacific (NFIP), operating on the premise "that whatever happens in one part of the Pacific Ocean affects the whole ocean" (Teaiwa 1994, 101). It has now become clear that the US military's nuclear tests in the Pacific have affected both human and marine life, which share coral reefs as a habitat.

It is neither a coincidence nor a contradiction that the rise of the Nuclear Age and of systems ecology took place at the same time and place. The US Atomic Energy Commission funded surveys of the radioactive aftermath of its nuclear tests in the Pacific conducted, among others, by Eugene and Howard Odum, who later became well-known for their contributions to systems ecology. They departed for Eniwetok Atoll in 1955 shortly after the US military Operation Ivy had destroyed the island of Elugelab, and developed what they call "radiation ecology" (DeLoughrey 2013, 169). In 1955, the Odums published an article about the measurable effects of radioactive fallout on marine habitats and especially coral reef communities, embracing the "unique opportunity ... for critical assays of the effects of radiations due to fission products *on whole populations and entire ecosystems in the field*" (1955, 291). Systems ecology is based on the assumption that habitats can be isolated and analyzed as closed ecosystems (Odum 1953). Elizabeth DeLoughrey argues that isolated islands or atolls such as Bikini or Eniwetok served as ideal laboratories and sites for ecosystem research in the 1950s. Following this logic, the distant Marshall Islands "became a nuclear colony under President Truman's doctrine of oceanic colonialism" (DeLoughrey 2013, 169). The US military not only controlled the 846 square miles of land, but also three million square miles of aquatic territory belonging to Micronesia.

The Bikini Atoll, located in the northern part of the Marshall Islands, boasts a turbulent colonial history (D'Arcy 2006). The islands—Majõl in the local language—were renamed for Western audiences after British captain John Marshall, who visited them in 1766. The Atoll was mapped in 1825 for the first time by the circumnavigator and explorer Otto von Kotzebue and officially colonized by the German Empire in 1886 as the Eschscholtz Islands (Deutsche Kolonialgesellschaft 1920, 210). The lagoon covers an area of about 600 square meters and is up to 60 meters deep. During the First World War, the Marshall Islands were occupied by Japanese troops; they were conquered by the USA in 1944. The two largest islands of the atoll, Bikini—Bigini in the local language—and Enyu, have been the home to 167 and 29 Indigenous people respectively until 1946, when all Marshall islanders were resettled by the US authorities to the smaller, low-food, and up until then uninhabited, Rongerik Atoll.

In order to understand how the long-term series of nuclear tests by the US military has affected the atoll and its marine environment, it is important to examine how atolls evolve. Atolls are ring-shaped coral reefs that rise above the sea and enclose a lagoon. Corals are polyps living in colonies symbiotically with an algae called zooxanthellae, exchanging photosynthesized oxygen and nutrients. Their preferred environment is shallow water, but coral reefs can also be found in deeper seas. The building of a coral reef takes millions of years. The first coral reefs were formed in the Ordovician period about 485 million years ago, and have undergone several phases of extinction. Reefs recover very slowly, and highly diverse reefs especially take a long time to rebuild themselves. Recovery rates range from a few million up to 140 million years (Leinfelder 2019). Coral reefs can be found in the Mediterranean Sea as well as in the Atlantic and in the Indian Ocean. However, the Pacific Ocean has the most extensive and diverse coral reefs, notably the Great Barrier Reef northeast of Australia.

Corals have fascinated people since antiquity, because the soft, colorful polyps die off on land, leaving behind their hard skeleton. In Greek philosophy of nature, corals were praised above all for their mutability, and became regarded as "artist[s] in metamorphosis" (Bredekamp 2019, 62). Corals were collected, made into jewelry, and found their way into pre-modern cabinets of curiosities as well as scientific mineral displays. They have long been regarded as plants due to their symbiotic relationship with algae and, like the related sea anemones, have been classified as flower animals (*Anthozoa*). One of the first empirical studies on coral species was Henry Baker's *Attempt Towards a Natural History of the Polype* (1743). The naturalist Baker conducted microscopic studies of the morphology and growth of native species.[3] He observed the way the polyps—living specimens that he kept alive in glasses filled with seawater—move and reproduce by separation:

> I have been examining them daily, both with and without the Help of Glasses, and have attended with the strictest Care to all their little Motions, Contractions, Extensions, and different Postures, as well as to their more extraordinary Properties, that I might thereby be enabled to give some reasonable account of their Structure and Disposition. (Baker 1743, 8)

The fact that corals build reefs through mineralization and the secretion of their hard exoskeleton became increasingly clear in the nineteenth century, when world-traveling naturalists such as Alexander von Humboldt were focusing on marine environments. He argued that in the oceans, which after all cover almost three-quarters of the entire surface of the Earth, a richer abundance of organic life could be found than on the mainland (Humboldt 1845, 330).

To study corals in their natural habitat and not in a laboratory, the zoologist Christian Gottfried Ehrenberg undertook a journey to the Red Sea in 1823 and published his treatise *Die Corallenthiere*

3 Baker refers to the Dutch naturalist Antoni van Leeuwenhoek (1633–1723), who constructed hundreds of microscopes and also investigated protozoa and bacteria.

des roten Meeres in 1834. Because corals die quickly when they are removed from their natural habitat—constantly moving seawater—the naturalist was inevitably forced to go to where they live. Ehrenberg therefore settled in a tent on a Red Sea beach and collected living corals in water-filled glasses and buckets, without exposing them to air. To do so he combined his scientific interest in taxonomy with a field study of the situatedness of the living organism—what later became the essence of marine ecology. Ehrenberg investigated the reproduction of corals by complete or incomplete splitting off (budding) and observed that richly branched coral trunks are created by incomplete separation of polyps from the mother trunk. They form what he called "Familienvereine," i.e., family associations (Ehrenberg 1834, 24). In the life sciences and beyond, corals symbiotically living in colonies have become a symbol for the cohabitation of different species in a shared habitat—showing similarities with human collectives (Helmreich 2015, 51).

The naturalist Charles Darwin investigated the structure and distribution of coral reefs in the Indian and Pacific Oceans during his circumnavigation between 1832 and 1836. He visited Tahiti, Mauritius, and the Cocos (Keeling) Islands. At the latter he stayed 12 days to make observations. Darwin was strongly interested in global geology at that time and developed a theory about the evolution of coral reefs, positing their development through successive subsidence states of foundering volcanic islands (Rosen 1982).[4] He differentiated between fringing reefs, barrier reefs, and atolls and published his observations in two short statements in 1837 and 1839, and later in length in his 1842 treatise *The Structure and Distribution of Coral Reefs*. In this book, Darwin is full of admiration and excitement for the lagoon-forming coral reefs and especially for the polyps that do the work of building these reefs against the immense power of the sea:

4 It is reported that Darwin took Charles Lyell's *Principles of Geology* from 1830 on his journey.

> The naturalist will feel this astonishment more deeply after having examined the soft and almost gelatinous bodies of these apparently insignificant creatures, and when he knows that the solid reef increases only on the outer edge, which day and night is lashed by the breakers of an ocean never at rest. (Darwin 1842, 1)

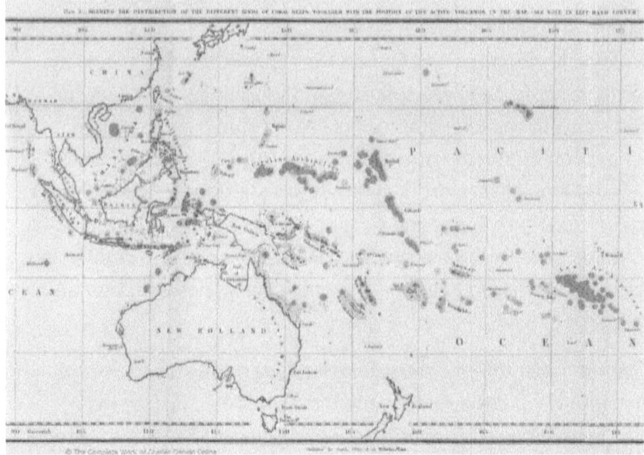

[Fig. 1] Map detail of the distribution of coral reefs in the Indian and Pacific Oceans (Source: Charles Darwin. *The Structure and Distribution of Coral Reefs: Being the First Part of the Geology of the Voyage of the Beagle 1842*, Plate III)

Darwin searched for living organisms at the boundary between land and water to show the stages of transition from soft polyps into solid limestone (Rosen 1982, 521). Nevertheless, the exploration of the actual habitat of corals was carried out by means of deep sounding and plumb lines coated with tallow. Therein, small fragments of corals are pressed in, which can then be brought to the water surface. Darwin was convinced that dead coral material combined with calcite forms the basis for all reefs.

However, on his crossing of the Pacific, Darwin did not set a foot on the Marshall Islands and Bikini Atoll, which Kotzebue had mapped in 1825. His hope that someone would undertake drillings in some of the Pacific or Indian atolls to prove his subsidence theory became true in 1951 and 1952, when the American Atomic Energy Commission and the Los Alamos Scientific Laboratory drilled three holes on Eniwetok Atoll, Northern Marshall Islands, as part of a test program (Rosen 1982, 519). The drilling was conducted to extract geological and biological samples from deep sediment layers, now deposited in the US National Museum. These drillings went down more than 4,000 feet. Further drillings were carried out on Bikini Atoll. As the geologist and paleontologist William Storrs Cole (1957, 744) claims: "These holes for the first time give valuable information about the deeper subsurface geology of a coral atoll. … Information of this sort has been desired by geologists and biologists since the time of Darwin." Next to nuclear testing and deep sea drilling, another way of colonizing the ocean is attempting to penetrate its depths in order to take possession of its inhabitants and resources.

24° 40′ N, 77° 55′ W: Andros Barrier Reef—Coral Extraction and Underwater Laboratories

Between 1923 and 1930, the marine biologist Roy Waldo Miner, who coined the term "marine ecology" in 1911, led field expeditions to the Andros Barrier Reef in the Bahamas. At that time Miner was curator of marine life and living invertebrates at the American Museum of Natural History in New York and was commissioned to create a diorama of the dazzling underwater world of coral reefs for the museum. Like Darwin, he had a strong passion for coral reefs—"world-builders" in his understanding:

> The reef-building coral polyp, with its associates, has probably produced the most significant and conspicuous results of all the lower inhabitants of the sea. Its castellated structures of limestone may rise from depths to twenty or thirty fathoms to the ocean surface, and, in the case of

> the Great Barrier Reef of Australia, extend for more than fourteen hundred miles in lengths. … As world-builders, the coral and its associates have taken part in the construction of many oceanic islands forming the abodes of men, and during past geologic ages, were an important source of the continental limestone deposits of the world. (Miner [1931] 1933, 3)

Despite his admiration for the world-building activity of corals, Miner did not hesitate to extract large quantities of coral material, primarily of the elkhorn, staghorn and fan species, from the great Bahaman Coral Reef Group—he speaks enthusiastically of 40 tons, from the sea, bleaching it in the air, that is, letting the polyps die—and shipping these to New York. In a museum guide Miner describes the method of bleaching and dying the polyps in detail: "This process consists in keeping the surface of the corals wet until the thin outer layer of animal tissue decays and sloughs off, leaving the white limestone skeleton exposed" ([1931] 1933, 2). He starts his report on the four expeditions to the Caribbean Sea by recalling the stages of excavation, transport and building a replica in three sentences only—giving them a sense of drama anyway:

> Forty tons of coral trees growing on the ocean floor, bathed in the crystal waters of tropic seas, three fathoms below the surface, amid waving sea plumes and schools of brilliantly colored fishes between their branches!
>
> Forty tons of corals ripped from the heart of a hundred-mile submarine forest on tinted limestone, hauled to a snowy beach, bleached, embedded in sponge clippings, packed in huge crates, and shipped to the American Museum!
>
> Forty tons of coral rising from the floor of the Hall of the Ocean Life, their serrated branches interlaced as of old and once more invested with the delicate hues that gave them their pristine beauty, while above them again spreads the

mirroring quicksilver of a simulated watery surface beneath the blue of a painted tropic sky! (Miner [1931] 1933, 2)

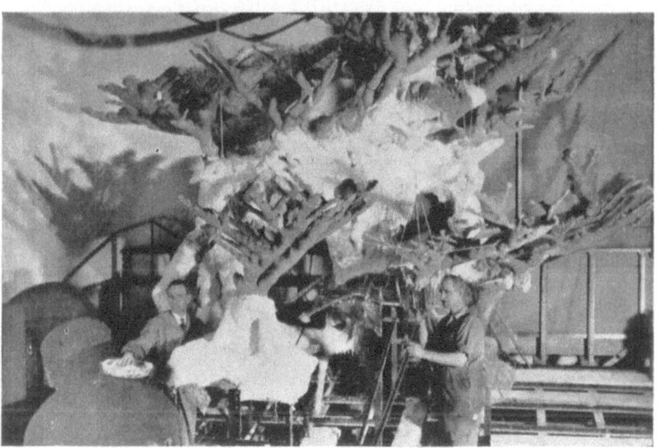

[Fig. 2] Modeling a Coral Reef with the Help of Steel Supports (Source: Miner [1931] 1933, 8)

Without doubt, Miner is proud of the artificially reconstructed lifelike coral reef in the Hall of Ocean Life. It does not occur to him to regret being responsible for the death of so many living polyps. On the contrary: the triple repetition of the amount of captured coral material underlines his will to take possession of this extremely species-rich habitat. In addition, his contribution is illustrated with a number of photographs documenting the successful progress of the enterprise, from the extraction of corals at the Bahaman Great Coral Reef group through the display of the captured samples to the presentation of the built replica reef at the Museum of National History in New York. Miner celebrates the appropriation of 40 tons of coral material as a scientific achievement staged in a way that appeals to the public. In this undertaking, the field, the lab, the museum, and the archive as the main places of doing science in the Western world are closely tied in a network of appropriation and knowledge production.

Even at that time, it was common practice for marine biologists to remove marine life from its natural habitat in order to study it. But Miner's team was also equipped with underwater photo and film cameras to observe the marine life *in situ*: "We had three undersea cameras, two for black, and one for color film," as Miner explains, and "There were also two helmets and pumps, which thus enabled two persons to get under the sea at a time" (1933, 13). To do so, one diver had to operate the camera and record images. The expedition also had an under-sea tube, James Ernest Williamson's *Photosphere*, at their disposal (Elias 2019, 75)—a sort of submarine laboratory made of steel and with a "plate glass window," enabling people inside the tube to observe the marine life from a dry distance (Miner [1931] 1933, 4). Among the participants of the third expedition was also Chris Olsen of the Museum modeling staff. As Miner reported, Olsen made "sketches with oil colors directly from nature, undersea, at a depth of fifteen to twenty feet" (1933, 13). Capturing the true colors of the various corals underwater was regarded as essential for achieving a lifelike replication in the Museum's waterless diorama.

Miner in fact believed that the diorama was "a record of living beings in their natural state and environment, depicted in their proper relations to their surroundings, and emphasizing the truth that the real unit in nature is the association rather than the individual" ([1931] 1933, 9). However, this replica of a Caribbean Sea coral reef is a completely artificial environment, empty of life—a perfect simulation framed by scientific practices of extraction, sorting, classification, storing, and display. Eight tons of steel was necessary to support the corals and other marine life in exactly the same position they had taken in their natural habitat. The creation of the two-level diorama had become possible thanks to underwater technologies and artificial submarine environments enabling scientists to observe marine life at a close distance. Underwater expeditions including photographic recordings of marine life in their habitat "reinforced colonial legacies and gendered perspectives on diving and filming" (Torma 2013, 19). The *Andros Coral Reef Diorama* is still in its place in the Museum's Hall of Ocean Life.

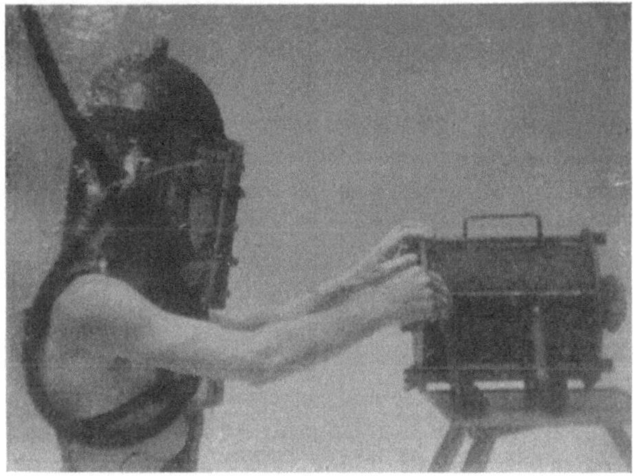

[Fig. 3] Underwater filming (Source: Miner [1931] 1933, 10)

In the twentieth century, submarines and other artificial underwater environments offered renewed options for colonizing the ocean and appropriating its resources. Diving techniques and underwater laboratories also played an important role in the scientific exploration of the ocean by marine biologists, testing the adaptability of humans to extreme conditions of high atmospheric pressure and artificial atmospheres. The development of underwater laboratories increased after World War II, when the campaigns for the conquest of outer space required practical experience with tools and materials for keeping humans alive under extreme environmental conditions. Underwater laboratories provided controlled artificial spaces that served as bases for observations of deeper marine environments and as test sites for space-colonizing programs of industrialized countries of the "Global North". Between 1965 and 1980, more than 65 such enclosed artificial environments were built that temporarily occupied the ocean floor (Mesinovic 2013, 265).

From 15 February, 1969 onwards, two physical oceanographers and two geologists spent 60 days in the underwater laboratory *Tektite I*, submerged 49 feet deep in the Greater Lamashur Bay near St. John, one of the United States Virgin Islands. The first civilian underwater laboratory on the seafloor of the Caribbean Sea was tightly connected to the US space program, treating the ocean as an alien environment analogous to "outer space." Adapting humans to hostile environments was crucial to crewed spaceflight programs and designs for orbital space stations. Reports on that mission, partly financed by the US Office of Naval Research and the National Aeronautics and Space Administration (NASA), declare that its only justification "was to study the behavior of an 'isolated' group of men subject to the 'stress' of an 'hostile' environment" (Mesinovic 2013, 268). In the same year, a German underwater laboratory was set up submerged about 75 feet deep in the cold water of the North Sea northeast of Heligoland Island. The crew consisted of two biologists, a professional diver, and a physician from the German Space Agency (DFVRL), who connected marine biology to space flight research.

Underwater research and outer space programs share an interest in testing the adaptability of humans to enclosed artificial environments. An article published in 1969 in the popular West German diving magazine *Delphin* makes this connection explicit by claiming that "astronauts and aquanauts have much in common" (quoted in Mesinovic 2013, 269). However, the aquanauts at the underwater laboratory *Helgoland* faced numerous technical problems, such as struggles with heating the living space and drying the diving suits. The underwater laboratory was not designed for permanent habitation: its main objective was to collect data from both the marine environment and the scientists who lived there for a certain period of time. When, in 1970, *Tektite II* was designed as an international underwater laboratory, two members of the German *Helgoland* crew were among the participants of this new mission, explicitly "dedicated to behavioral research in the context of space flight" (Mesinovic 2013, 272). Conquering the depths of the ocean and exploring outer space follow the same geopolitical agenda to colonize thus far unreachable territories and to come into possession of their resources.

First attempts to explore the ocean with the help of submarines were undertaken in 1800 by the American engineer Robert Fulton. His *Nautilus*, almost six and a half meters long, was built at the Perrier shipyard in Rouen, France. The iron construction covered with copper plates had a depth rudder for steering and was moved under water by a hand-cranked propeller. Upward and downward lifting of the boat was regulated by flooding and emptying the hollow iron keel. Fulton's *Nautilus* already had torpedoes on board and was designed as a warship. It is therefore not surprising that Jules Verne, in *20,000 Leagues under the Sea*, named Captain Nemo's submarine *Nautilus*. Verne's main protagonist, descendant of an Indian royal family having studied in England, uses torpedoes to attack ships of colonial empires loaded with raw materials that have been extracted from mines in his homeland. However, Verne's *Nautilus* is not only a warship, it is also a mobile asylum for guerilla fighters and an underwater laboratory. In the science fiction novel, thanks to the artificial environment of the submarine, Captain Nemo and his followers are able to colonize the deep sea and the seabed using its rich resources of fish and sea plants for sustaining their life. Equipped with diving suits and breathing apparatuses, the men roam the deep sea and the seabed, hunting for fish and other "treasures of the sea."

When Verne published the novel in 1869, the world's oceans were already being eagerly mapped by physical oceanographers using soundings and plumb lines to penetrate their depths. In 1868, 1869, and 1870 zoologist Charles Wyville Thomson led three deep-sea dredging expeditions in the Atlantic. The results of these expeditions were released in 1873 under the telling title

 The Depths of the Sea (Thomson 1873). Among similar attempts to explore the ocean's depths the British *Challenger Expedition* from 1873 to 1876, led by the physical oceanographer John Murray and again Thomson, stands out because for the first time, "continuous series of hydrographic and zoological deep-sea expeditions" (Miner 1911, 208) were undertaken. The amount of data and the compilation of samples that were gathered during the expedition exceeded all previous similar attempts, aiming for a "completeness, totality and closure never before known" (Höhler 2002, 126).

The more soundings were carried out, the more accurate the information about the deep sea became. Murray applied the term "deep" to "those areas of the seafloor where the depth exceeds 3,000 fathoms or three geographical miles" (1910, 619). At that time 56 such deeps were known, four of them exceeding a depth of 5,000 fathoms.[5] More so, the *Challenger Expedition* found "that living organisms were to be found everywhere in the ocean, from the surface waters down to depths of three or four geographical miles" (Murray 1910, 618). In his influential 1910 article, Murray coined the term "biosphere"[6] (1910, 618) and advocated the idea that deep-sea exploration could provide insights into the past history of the planet and its circles of living and non-living matter. He was also interested in the structure and origin of coral reefs and islands, criticizing Darwin's assumptions about that topic (Murray 1879-80). Thus, coral reefs play an important role in the establishment of marine biology and, even more so, of ecological thought. Coral reefs are associations of organisms that are in steady exchange with their aquatic environment to sustain their life and that of other marine inhabitants. This is why they are vulnerable habitats: coral reefs are not closed

5 Three thousand fathoms equals 5,486 meters. See also Murray and Hjort (1912, 133ff).

6 The term was adopted by Vladimir Vernatsky's 1926 book *The Biosphere*, first published in Russian.

ecosystems—rather, they are filters for the permanent exchange of matter and energy in the ocean.

28° 45′ N, 88° 18′ W: Deepwater Horizon Platform—Colonizing and Polluting the Deep Sea

On April 20, 2010, the sky over *Deepwater Horizon,* a drilling platform set up in the Gulf of Mexico, was covered by black smoke. The platform, which was operated by the companies Transocean and BP, and was supposed to excavate 5,500 meter-deep oil reserves, 4,000 meters below the seabed, had caught fire. Two days later, it sank. In the months following this disaster, large quantities of oil leaked, collected at the surface of the ocean, and reached the surrounding coasts, harming the habitats of marine and coastal dwellers. The deep-sea coral reefs and reefs in the mesophotic zone in the Gulf of Mexico were also affected by oil particles and chemical dispersants, creating a so-called dirty blizzard that showered the seafloor (Etnoyer, Wickes and Silva 2016). Recordings of oil washed up on the coasts, of oil-covered seabirds, dead fish, and marine mammals, aerial images showing the oil spill, as well as images of high amounts of oil dispersed in the aquatic space taken by underwater cameras, went around the world. The underwater images show how special ships and remotely operated diving robots tried to close the leak and prevent further oil leakage. The ecological disaster unmasked the desire to wrest control of the bottom of the ocean as a toxic phantasma.

This was not the only disaster that happened as a result of the attempts to explore and appropriate the deeper grounds of the ocean by making them a site for deep-sea mining or other late-capitalist efforts to extract saleable materials from the seabed. A colonization of this underwater territory in the service of imperialist "petromodernity" (LeMenager 2014) has long since begun.

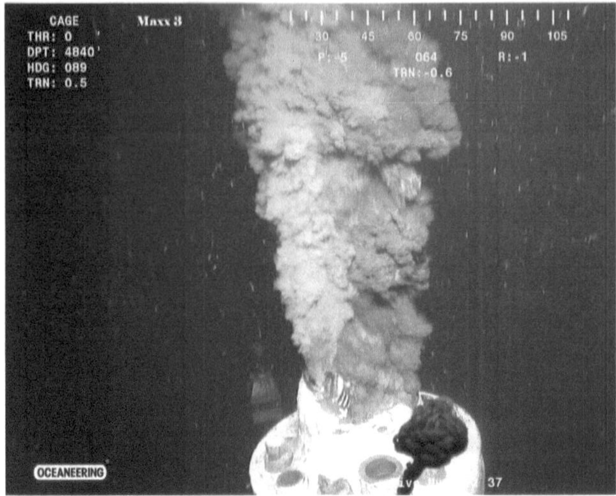

[Fig. 4] Hydrocarbons escaping on June 3, 2010 from the end of the riser tube after BP *Deepwater Horizon* oil spill (Source: Marcia K. McNutt et al. 2012. "Review of Flow Rates Estimates of the *Deepwater Horizon Oil Spill.*" *PNAS* 109(50): 20260-20267, fig. 5)

Exactly under the North Pole, a Russian flag was rammed into the seabed in 2007, in order to claim ownership of the area, should it turn out that mineral resources can be found there. It seems to be a strange coincidence that, in 2011, the Canadian company Nautilus Minerals—named after Nemo's submarine—achieved an initial license for seabed mining in territorial waters from Papua New Guinea (Hessler 2019, 36).[7] The ocean has become an economically exploitable resource, a geopolitically contested space—and a deposit of globally circulating, toxic atomic, chemical, and other human-made waste that alters critical biogeochemical processes on Earth with uncertain results. The deep sea and the seabed are not a distant and strange realm any more. After

7 The curator Stefanie Hessler refers to material presented in the video "Prospect Ocean" (2018) by artist and researcher Armin Linke. A web series entitled *What is deep sea mining?* by the online channel Inhabitants explicitly discusses environmental degradation and capitalist extractivism.

centuries of exploration, the ocean is gradually losing its secrets, and also its treasures.

Similar to outer space, the ocean was long considered synonymous with the unknown. "Up to that time the bottom of what sailors call 'blue water' was as unknown to us as is the interior of any of the planets of our system" (Maury 1858, 114),[8] writes US Navy Lieutenant Matthew Fontaine Maury in 1858, in the eighth edition of his seminal scientific contribution to oceanography and metrology, *Explanation and Sailing Directions to Accompany the Wind and Current Charts*. Maury draws a direct line between the inner space of deep sea and the interior of planets in outer space concerning their inaccessibility and strangeness. To change this situation, he engaged in the new field of physical oceanography and organized, in 1853, the first international maritime congress in Brussels to establish a systematic observation of global wind and current distribution (Höhler 2002, 123).

Maury was interested in bathometry and the geography of the seafloor, but no less in deep-sea marine life, which he valued as essential for the physical balance between land and sea: "Every specimen from the bottom of the deep sea is, therefore, to be regarded as a valuable contribution to the sources of human knowledge" (Maury 1854, 302). Physical oceanographers like Maury already recognized the importance of the ocean and marine life for the ecological balance of the Earth. Because of their ability to absorb salt dissolved in water and to secrete it again as lime deposit, he attributed especially to coral reefs the important task "of assisting in given circulation to the ocean, and of helping to regulate the climates of the Earth" (Maury 1854, 186). Among his scientific fellows was Christian Gottfried Ehrenberg, who not only investigated the coral reefs in the Red Sea, but also

8 A similar formulation can be found in the sixth edition (1854) on page 224. The first edition appeared in 1851.

 proved "with his microscope" (Maury 1854, 133) the circulation of air between the equator and the northern hemisphere.[9]

Maury explicitly acknowledged the importance of dead deep-sea specimens for regulating the saltiness of the sea and thereby "the physical economy of the universe" (1854, 301). He saw the ocean and its marine life as an immense global filter, "a vast chemical bath in which the solid parts of the earth were washed, filtered and precipitated again as solid matter, but in a new form, and with fresh properties" (Maury 1854, 301). The deep space of the ocean became itself an epistemic milieu, a medium from which knowledge about the global circles of matter and energy and, even more so, the ecology of the entire planet, can be extracted. Extracting knowledge here means collecting specimens and comparing data, for instance about the distribution of little shells transported by ocean currents over long distances. According to Maury,

> They are facts that concern our planet and touch the well-being or the rightly knowing of its inhabitants; and, therefore, renewed attention to this subject of deep-sea soundings, and the specimens of the bottom that may be brought up, cannot fail to be regarded but with increasing interest. (Maury 1854, 302)

Oceanography therefore was, at that time, the most appropriate science to develop an ecological view on the interdependence of life at land and in the sea and to reveal the importance of the ocean and its inhabitants for the circulation of matter and energy on Earth.

Before submarines and remotely operated diving robots entered the depths of the ocean, deep-sea sounding was the privileged technology to extract samples from the seafloor. Submarines have been reaching out for the deep sea since the middle of

9 Throughout the book, Maury refers several times to Ehrenberg's research on air circulation.

the twentieth century. To date, a significant purpose of such undertakings is to measure the deepest point of the seabed. On 23 January, 1960, the submarine *Trieste*, with oceanographers Jacques Piccard and Don Walsh on board, reached the Mariana Trench in the western Pacific for the first time. They determined the deepest point on the sea floor at 10,916 meters. Another submarine, the *Nereus*, reached a low point of 10,902 meters there in 2009. Furthermore, in 2007, Google launched a new tool called Google Ocean, which is intended to facilitate the localization of coral reefs, such as the Great Barrier Reef northeast of Australia, or the location of shipwrecks and marine archaeological sites. Their shared interest is to map the ocean as a territory that is accessible either by means of submarine technologies, including optical systems or satellite navigation systems (GPS) and computer graphics. However, no insights are given with this Google application into the real depth and composition of the sea, or any information about rising temperatures and sea levels, or dying coral reefs as the main effects of recent anthropogenic global warming (Helmreich 2011).

The ocean, essential for global ecology, has become a major site of ecological crisis. In 2019, a team led by the American financier and retired naval officer Victor Vescovo, on board the *Limiting Factor*, also measured a depth of 10,928 meters in the Mariana Trench. The task of this mission was to carry out detailed sonar measurements to map this shadowy realm. Vescovo said that in addition to four previously unknown species, he found two plastic bags on that spot at the bottom of the ocean.[10] Images of these findings were widely distributed in the media to prove that man-made litter has even reached the deepest place underwater.

Plastic waste has colonized the ocean. As media theorist Jennifer Gabrys points out, waste "is the stratum of the past in the present that is often overlooked" (2013, 132). Susan Freinkel

10 On May 13, 2019, many newsreel channels distributed the news worldwide, *The Times* and the BBC among others.

 defines plastic as an umbrella term for a "cornucopia of materials, a dazzling variety of the synthetica" (2011, 18). Starting in the first decades of the twentieth century and accelerated during World War II, new polymers where invented as byproducts of the growing petroleum industry. The emergence of plastics, which result from the extraction of fossil fuels from the Earth, is intertwined with the flows of organic materials that are themselves remainders of earlier geological formations. Today, plastic is more and more considered an undesired burden that challenges and destroys ecosystems on land, as well as in the ocean. It has become common knowledge now that synthetic materials such as plastics are toxic to environments, and to living organisms if they enter their metabolisms.

Plastic deposits not only in landfills on land, but circulates also in rivers and seas. In the ocean, plastic waste is moved by wind stress and surface currents and is assembled in patches, such as the so-called Pacific garbage patch—a giant floating waste-island in the North Pacific that is said to have a diameter measured in thousands of kilometers: a territory as big as Texas. As observers of floating garbage in the North Pacific and elsewhere noticed, the vortex does not have a static form. It is a dynamic assemblage that has no boundaries and cannot be measured. Furthermore, the patch "isn't filled with floes of debris"—instead, it consists of "gazillions of tiny bits and pieces suspended, like the flakes in a snow globe, throughout the water column, from the surface to the visible depth" (Freinkel 2011, 243). These tiny bits and pieces of plastic items represent a first state of decomposition, called abiotic degradation, which results in fragmentation and size reduction, lower molecule weight, and decrease in tensile strength. The states of decomposition range from micro to nano scale. Pieces of plastic, however big or small they are, sink into the deep sea and deposit on the sea floor, which has become the final resting place for many kinds of man-made litter.

Micro-plastics interact with their new marine environment in different ways: some may be overgrown by marine life such as corals, others may be incorporated by filter- and sediment-feeding organisms, at times being expelled back into the water, and yet others sediment on the seafloor (Leinfelder and Asunção Ivar do Sul 2019, 151). Plastics are a large part of man-made techno-fossils, many of them traveling through the ocean to eventually store on the seafloor, where they become a useful stratigraphic tool for indicating Anthropocene sedimentary deposits. Beside atomic fallout plastic waste has become one of the most massive effects in terms of human alteration of environments and habitats.

Especially in regions of military impact such as Bikini Atoll and Johnston Atoll in the Pacific, or Diego Garcia Island in the Indian Ocean, radioactive and chemical wastes proliferate, turning atolls into environments hostile to biotic life. Massive coral dredging and deep drilling undertaken on these atolls destroys the marine ecosystem of reef communities and beyond. Such toxic environments, which can be found throughout the planet, make up what artists Anca Benera and Arnold Estefán call the "debrisphere," the devastating environmental "effects of technological warfare and its supporting infrastructure on aquatic and terrestrial landscapes, non-human species, and local communities" (Fowkes and Fowkes 2018, 19).

Entangled Geographies and Anthropocene Histories

A diffractive reading of Anthropocene histories of coral reefs has revealed the long fascination with corals and coral reefs in Western science and art. More than a species with many facets, corals are word-builders that create habitats for other species and shape the geography of the Earth. Moreover, coral reefs incorporate the very idea of sedimentation, including processes of materialization—steady currents of materials and transitions between the living and the nonliving. They are living archives of the world—archives of the future world and its traces of anthropogenic extraction, pollution, and extinction. Western colonization not only violently appropriates territories of land and sea, but establishes extraction as a principle that also informs scientific theories and practices. Undoubtedly, the attempts to colonize the ocean have many facets, but ever far reaching consequences for all life on Earth.

Due to the increase in water temperature massive events of coral bleaching, namely in the Great Barrier Reef, are approaching in ever shorter time intervals. A new wave of species extinction is expected by marine scientists, which will have lasting effects on ecologies worldwide. To avert another mass extinction of reef communities, it is not enough to experiment with more robust coral species as supporters of an "assisted evolution" inspired by Darwin's theory, or to resettle coral species in colder marine environments, which would be just another act of colonizing aquatic habitats. The main questions remain: What are the ecological effects of colonial politics and allied colonizing scientific practices? What does it mean not to colonize the ocean, to invent other modes of experimentation, research, representation, archiving, and storytelling? To create sustainable futures we have to decolonize the ocean and all its inhabitants. As Joshua Schuster points out, "life and death of coral overlap with indigenous struggles for decolonization and oceanic solidarity in the face of rising seas" (2019, 91).

This article proposed the term "epistemic milieu" to envision the interdependencies between different spaces, technologies, and practices of colonial knowledge production in the lab, the field, the museum, and the archive. This notion aims to criticize the extraction principle at work in capitalist deep-sea mining, entrepreneurial expeditions and—although less "visible"—in scientific investigations that involve collecting samples etc. from marine habitats. All of these practices are different, nevertheless entangled modes of colonization carried out through Western knowledge production and appropriation. A dispersed genealogy of encounters with marine species and their habitats allows us to revise the established Western geographies of knowledge production and to create alternative modes of being in the world.

The work for this essay was inspired by conversations with participants at the Modeling the Pacific conference held at the University of California, Santa Barbara in October 2019. My special thanks to Christina Vagt. I am also grateful to the Cluster of Excellence "Matters of Activity. Image, Space, Material" at the Humboldt University of Berlin for its generous support.

References

Baker, Henry. 1743. *An Attempt Towards a Natural History of the Polype: In a Letter to Martin Folkes, Esq., President of the Royal Society.* London: Printed for M. Dodsley.

Barad, Karen. 2007. *Meeting the Universe Halfway: Quantum Physics and the Entanglement of Matter and Meaning*, Durham, NC: Duke University Press.

Bredekamp, Horst. 2019. *Darwin's Corals: A New Model of Evolution and the Tradition of Natural History.* Translated by Elizabeth Clegg. Berlin: De Gruyter.

Bonneuil, Christoph, and Jean-Baptiste Fressoz. 2015. *The Shock of the Anthropocene: The Earth, History and Us.* New York: Verso.

Cole, W. Storrs. 1957. *Larger Foraminifera from Eniwetok Atoll Drill Holes, Bikini Atolls and Nearby Marshall Islands.* US Geological Survey Professional Paper 260-V.

D'Arcy, Paul. 2006. *The People of the Sea: Environments, Identity, and History in Oceania.* Honolulu: University of Hawaii Press.

Darwin, Charles. 1842. *The Structure and Distribution of Coral Reefs: Being the First Part of the Geology of the Voyage of the Beagle (1832–1836).* London: Smith, Elder & Co.

DeLoughrey, Elizabeth M. 2013. "The Myth of Isolates. Ecosystem Ecologies in the Nuclear Pacific." *Cultural Geographies* 20 (2): 176–82.

Deutsche Kolonialgesellschaft, ed. 1920. *Deutsches Koloniallexikon*, vol. 1. Accessed March 9, 2020. http://www.ub.bildarchiv-dkg.uni-frankfurt.de/Bildprojekt/Lexikon /Standardframeseite.php?suche=Bikini.

Ehrenberg, Christian Gottfried. 1834. *Die Corallenthiere des rothen Meeres: Physiologisch untersucht und systematisch verzeichnet.* Berlin: Druckerei der Königlichen Akademie der Wissenschaften.

Elias, Ann. 2019. *Coral Empire: Underwater Oceans, Colonial Tropics, Visual Modernity.* Durham, NC: Duke University Press.

Etnoyer, Peter J., Leslie N. Wickes, Mauricio Silva, et al. 2016. "Decline in Condition of Gorgonian Octocorals on Mesophotic Reefs in the Northern Gulf of Mexico: Before and After the Deepwater Horizon Oil Spill." *Coral Reefs* 35: 77–90.

Fowkes, Maja, and Reuben Fowkes. 2018. "Unsalvageable Futures of the Debrisphere." In *Debrisphere: Landscape as an Extension of the Military Imagination*, edited by Anca Benera and Arnold Estefán, 19–24. Bucharest: PUNCH.

Freinkel, Susan. 2011. *Plastic: A Toxic Love Affair*. New York: Houghton, Mifflin & Harcourt.

Gabrys, Jennifer. 2013. *Digital Rubbish: A Natural History of Electronics*. Ann Arbor: University of Michigan Press.

Helmreich, Stefan. 2011. "From Spaceship Earth to Google Ocean: Planetary Icons, Indexes, and Infrastructures." *Social Research* 78 (4): 211–42.

Helmreich, Stefan. 2015. *Sounding the Limits of Life: Essays in the Anthropology of Biology and Beyond*. Princeton: Princeton University Press.

Hessler, Stefanie. 2019. *Prospecting Ocean*. Cambridge: MIT Press.

Höhler, Sabine. 2002. "Depth Records and Ocean Volumes: Ocean Profiling by Sound Technology, 1850–1930." *History and Technology* 18 (2): 119–54.

Humboldt, Alexander von. 1845. *Kosmos: Entwurf einer physischen Weltbeschreibung*, vol. 1. Stuttgart: Cotta'scher Verlag.

Leinfelder, Reinhold. 2019. "Using the State of Reefs for Anthropocene Stratigraphy: An Ecostratigraphic Approach." In *The Anthropocene as a Geologic Time Unit: A Guide to the Scientific Evidence and Current Debate*, edited by Jan Zalasiewicz et al., 128–36. Cambridge: Cambridge University Press.

Leinfelder, Reinhold, and Juliana Asunção Ivar do Sul. 2019. "The Stratigraphy of Plastic and their Preservation in Geological Records." In *The Anthropocene as a Geologic Time Unit: A Guide to the Scientific Evidence and Current Debate*, edited by Jan Zalasiewicz et al., 147–55. Cambridge: Cambridge University Press.

LeMenager, Stephanie. 2014. *Living Oil: Petroleum Culture in the American Century*. Oxford: Oxford University Press.

Livingstone, David. 2003. *Putting Science in Place: Geographies of Scientific Knowledge*. Chicago: University of Chicago Press.

Maury, M. F. 1854. *Explanation and Sailing Directions to Accompany the Wind and Current Charts*, vol. 1. 6th enlarged edition. Philadelphia: E. C. and J. Biddle.

Maury, M. F. 1858. *Explanation and Sailing Directions to Accompany the Wind and Current Charts*, vol. 1. 8th enlarged edition. Washington, DC: William A. Harris

McNutt, Marcia K., Rich Camilli, Timothy J. Crone, et al. 2012. "Review of Flow Rates Estimates of the *Deepwater Horizon Oil Spill*." *PNAS* 109 (50): 20260–67.

Mesinovic, Sven Asim. 2013. "Reshaping Nature. Underwater Laboratories and Outer Space in West Germany and the United States." In *Wild Things: Nature and the Social Imagination*, edited by William Beinart, Karen Middleton, and Simon Pooley, 265–85. Cambridge: The White Horse Press.

Miner, Roy Waldo. 1911. "The Study of Marine Ecology and its Importance to the Fisheries." *Transactions of the American Fisheries Society* 40 (1): 207–17.

Miner, Roy Waldo. (1931) 1933. *Forty Tons of Coral*. Reprinted from National History Magazine for July–August, 1931. Guide Leaflet Series 78. New York: The Museum of Natural History.

Miner, Roy Waldo. 1933. *Diving in Coral Gardens*. Reprinted from National History Magazine for September–October, 1933. Guide Leaflet Series 80. New York: The Museum of Natural History.

Murray, John. 1879–80. "On the Structure and Origin of Coral Reefs and Islands." *Proceedings of the Royal Society of Edinburgh* 10 (107): 505–18.

Murray, John. 1910. "The Deep Sea." *The Scottish Geographical Magazine* 26 (12): 617–24.

Murray, John, and Johan Hjort. 1912. *The Depths of the Sea: A General Account of the Modern Science of Oceanography Based Largely on the Scientific Researches of the Norwegian Steamer "Michael Sars" in the North Atlantic*. London: Macmillan and Co.

Niedenthal, Jack. 2013. *For the Good of Mankind: A History of the People of Bikini and Their Islands*. 2nd edition. Marujo, Marshall Islands: Bravo Publishers.

Odum, Eugene P. 1953. *Fundamentals in Ecology*. Philadelphia: W. B. Saunders Company.

Odum, Howard T., and Eugene P. Odum. 1955. "Trophic Structure and Productivity of a Windward Coral Reef Community on Eniwetok Atoll." *Ecological Monographs* 25 (3): 291–320.

Rosen, Brian Roy. 1982. "Darwin, Coral Reefs, and Global Geology." *BioScience* 32 (6): 519–25.

Schuster, J. 2019. "Coral Cultures in the Anthropocene." *Cultural Studies Review* 25 (1): 85–102.

Teaiwa, Teresia K. 1994. "Bikinis and other s/pacific n/oceans." *The Contemporary Pacific* 6 (1): 87–109.

Thomson, Charles Wyville. 1873. *The Depths of the Sea: An Account on the General Results of the Dredging Cruises of H.M.SS. "Porcubine" and "Lightning."* London: Macmillan and Co.

Torma, Franziska. 2013. "Frontiers of Visibility: On Diving Mobility in Underwater Films." *Transfers* 3 (2): 24–46.

Waters, Colin N., Irka Hajdas, Catherine Jeandel, and Jan Zalasiewicz. 2019. "Artificial Radionuclide Fallout Signals." In *The Anthropocene as a Geologic Time Unit: A Guide to the Scientific Evidence and Current Debate*, edited by Jan Zalasiewicz, Colin N. Waters, Mark Williams, and Colin P. Summerhayes, 192–99. Cambridge: Cambridge University Press.

Zalasiewicz, Jan, Colin N. Waters, Anthony D. Barnosky, et al.; Members of the Anthropocene Working Group. 2015. "Colonization of the Americas, 'Little Ice Age' Climate, and Bomb-produced Carbon: Their Role in Defining the Anthropocene." *Anthropocene Review* 2 (2): 117–27.

Authors

Jakob Claus is a research associate at the Institute of Art and Visual Culture at Carl von Ossietzky University of Oldenburg. His research interests focus on technology and media theory, the formation of knowledge regimes, and colonial modes of epistemological exclusion.

Jörg Dünne is Professor of Romance Literatures at Humboldt University of Berlin. His fields of study are literatures in Spanish and French since early modernity, and his particular research interests include literature and cartography, catastrophism, and imaginations of deep time.

Réka Patrícia Gál is a PhD student at the Faculty of Information at the University of Toronto and a Fellow at the McLuhan Centre for Culture and Technology. Her main research interests are in feminist media theory, science and technology studies, environmental humanities, and anthropology of outer space.

Marie Heinrichs studies European Media Studies at the University of Potsdam. Her main areas of research interest include materialism(s), embodiment, physicality, feminist standpoint theory, critical theory of technology, and protest movements.

Petra Löffler is Professor of Theory and History of Contemporary Media at Carl von Ossietzky University of Oldenburg. Her particular research interests include media archeology, media ecologies, archival practices, and material culture.

Hannah Schmedes studies European Media Studies at the University of Potsdam and works at the Cluster of Excellence »Matters of Activity. Image, Space, Material« of Humboldt University of Berlin. Her research focusses on the correlation of biological and technical narratives about extraterrestrial colonialism and symbiosis.

Tomás J. Usón is a PhD student at the Institute for European Ethnology and IRI THESys at Humboldt University of Berlin. His main research interests are in risk and disaster studies, science and technology studies, urban anthropology and anthropological theory of time, memory and anticipation.

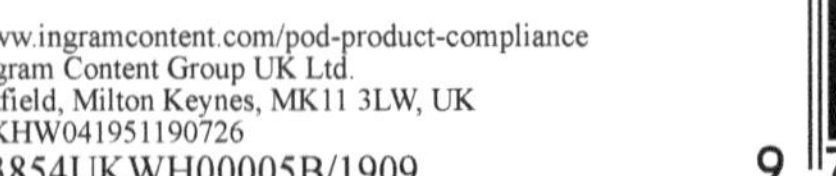

www.ingramcontent.com/pod-product-compliance
Ingram Content Group UK Ltd.
Pitfield, Milton Keynes, MK11 3LW, UK
UKHW041951190726
13854UKWH00005B/1909

9 783957 961891